KV-064-700

Grow!

Inspiration, Stories, and Practical Advice

REBBETZIN
S. FELDBRAND

I would like to express my thanks to Moshe Kaufman of Israel Bookshop; Elky Langer, editor; Zippy Thumim, layout and design; and Yocheved Krems, proofreader.

Copyright 2009 by S. Feldbrand

First edition — First impression / July 2009

Published by Lishmoa Lilmod U'Le'lamed

ALL RIGHTS RESERVED

Distributed by:

Israel Book Shop
501 Prospect Street
Lakewood, NJ 08701
Tel: (732) 901-3009
Fax: (732) 901-4012
e-mail: info@israelbookshoppublications.com

ISBN: 978-1-60091-104-0

Printed in Canada.

Jacket design and typesetting: Zippy Thumim

Grow!

Rabbi P. Hirschprung
230 Querbes
Montreal, Quebec
Tel. 514-276-9886

I was shown a book in English by Rebbetzin Feldbrand, relating to the topic of *tefillah*. She has assembled material which is certain to inspire its readers to heightened worship of Hashem, so that they are more acutely aware before Whom they stand in prayer. The various concepts on the power and importance of *tefillah* are sure to make prayers more meaningful for all. May Hashem accept our prayers for general and particular salvation. We should all merit to behold the Beis Ha'mikdash in its glory, in compassion, speedily in our days.

Translation of Rabbi Hirschprung, chief rabbi of Montreal's, *zt"l,* approbation to a previous sefer, *Towards Meaningful Prayer*, by Reb. S. Feldbrand.

Table of Contents

Preface..IX

The Importance of *Zerizus*...1

Personal Growth..77

Yetzer Hara: Friend or Foe...123

Shemiras Ha'lashon...183

Judging People Favorably...261

Preface

What is my task in this world? What does Hashem expect from me?

Man was created for the sole purpose of rejoicing in Hashem and ultimately deriving pleasure from the splendor of His presence (*Mesilas Yesharim*). To reach such a lofty level is an arduous task. The tools we were given are the mitzvos—but to reach that superlative goal, one must also perfect his inner self.

"*Derech eretz* preceded the Torah by twenty-six generations" (*Vayikra Rabbah* 9:3). Why? If a person lacks positive character traits, he will find it impossible to absorb the Torah properly. A person's spirit and character affects how he approaches his Torah learning. A truthful person will analyze and reason another way.

A humble person will reach different conclusions. If a person has learned Torah but does not possess refined character traits, his knowledge will evaporate, for Torah is inextricably intertwined with good character traits.

Perfection of character is the link between the mitzvos between man and man and those between man and Hashem.

When one keeps the mitzvos but lacks proper character traits, his mitzvos will be imperfect. Superior character enhances mitzvah performance.

Meeting life's challenges are easier for one who has good *middos*. So many contemporary problems are rooted in bad character. (Rav Aharon Yehudah Leib Steinman) This is why the Torah begins with the story of our Patriarchs and Matriarchs, and not with the first mitzvos commanded the Jewish nation: Hashem wanted us to learn to emulate the exemplary behavior of our forebears.

To achieve closeness to Hashem, then, requires working on perfecting our nature. Continuous growth requires that a person move forward at a steady pace. He must invest his energy and muster all the resources at his disposal to add to his personal advancement.

This *sefer* attempts to supply the wherewithal for that continued development. As with my other *seforim*, I have collected stories that throw light on the concepts presented for your edification.

Stories are helpful in many facets of our lives.

> *When students at the Philadelphia Yeshivah indicated that they did not adequately appreciate the shiur of Reb Mendel Kaplan, Rav Elya Svei, ztz"l, related that a talmid of Rav Chaim Volozhiner wanted to change yeshivah because Rav Chaim told too many stories; however, Reb Chaim didn't let him go. Years later the talmid said that the stories he heard helped him understand deep concepts in Kabbalah.*

"Here in Philadelphia you also have the opportunity to hear stories," Reb Elya concluded. *"To the extent that you listen to Reb Mendel's stories and thoughts, you will know how to live your lives."*

There was an elderly sexton who kept the Ponovezh Yeshivah spick-and-span. A Holocaust survivor, the man had lost his wife and children in the war, leaving him childless and desolate. His thoughts would often turn to the glorious prewar Torah world and his family that was no more. Sometimes his anguish was so overwhelming that he felt near collapse.

At those times, he would muster his resources and visit the Beis Yisroel of Gur. Disregarding the long line of people, he would enter through a back door and pour out his heart to the Rebbe, who always welcomed him warmly with the precise words of comfort and support that he needed. (Unfortunately, the Beis Yisroel was in the same situation, having lost all his children and grandchildren to the Nazis.)

One Simchas Torah, at the height of the celebrations at Ponovezh, the shammes was overcome by a thought. "If my children had survived they would certainly be dancing with these boys. Now they lie buried in some forsaken place in Europe."

The thought of his children and their disconnection from a Torah future broke his heart. He felt himself dissolving in a sea of pain. He sought out the Ponovezher Rav. Running to him, he cried, "Gevalt! Where *are my children? Why were they taken from me? They might have become great Torah scholars and devoted servants of Hashem! Why were they taken?"*

Those who heard his cries were shaken to their core. They knew that Rav Kalmanowitz, too, had lost his wife and all his children, except for Rav Avrohom, in the Holocaust.

Through his tears, the Rav declared, "One need not cry for them, for they died sanctifying Hashem's name. They are to be found in the most elevated spheres of the heavens, enjoying the greatest eternal pleasure. They are certainly learning together in the yeshivah up there.

"We really need to cry for ourselves. Where do we presently stand? What have we accomplished? How are we utilizing every moment of our lives? With each moment of learning Torah we can acquire immortality. Are we truly taking advantage of all the opportunities to be had?"

(Asara Nisyonos, pages 41–42)

Growth is a comprehensive catalog on self-improvement. Assembled between its covers are many tools to assist you in taking advantage of all the opportunities available. It contains practical advice that will enable you to capitalize on your strengths and improve your optimism and well-being. It is my hope that the information and guidelines for staying inspired and motivated will help you become a better you.

S. Feldbrand
Iyar 5769
Brooklyn, New York

The Importance of *Zerizus*

The Time Is Now

With our short lifespan, time is precious, and making the wisest use of our time in this world should be a high priority. Every mitzvah is a diamond, and as we pass through this world, we must actively seek them out to collect as many as we can. A person must serve Hashem with alacrity and seize countless good deeds. (*Maalos Ha'middos, Middah* 20)

A righteous individual traveled to visit a certain town. He stopped at the cemetery first, hoping to get a feel for the community. He was shocked to discover that the people of the town often died in their childhood and youth. Many reached the age of just thirty or forty, and a rare few attained the age of fifty.

Normally the man would have avoided such an ill-fated village, but since night had fallen, he was forced to remain. He hesitantly walked into the local shul, and was surprised to find it filled with people

1

learning Torah, reciting Tehillim, *and listening to the rabbi's Torah discourse. No one was chatting idly, gossiping, or indulging in mockery. There were people of all ages, including elderly men with white beards.*

When he questioned the townspeople, they willingly explained the mystery of the tombstones. Each child in the town was presented with a blank book at birth. As soon as he learned to write, he used the book to record his good deeds and the length of time each deed took, continuing this procedure throughout his life. When he died, the burial society took his life's book and added up the exact amount of time that he had spent performing mitzvos. It was that amount of time that was put on his headstone—because, they explained, only that time truly represents a person's life.

(Rabbi Lau on *Pirkei Avos*)

Zerizus includes everything that is required to make a mitzvah possible, such as eagerness, diligence, industry, and alacrity. *Zerizus* heads the list of good character traits: it helps us initiate all good deeds and utilize them to achieve the highest levels of spirituality. (*Orchos Tzaddikim*) The road to accomplishments is paved with *zerizus*, for it enables us to secure all that is valuable in this world. (*Daas Chochmah U'mussar*)

Food For Thought

"It is my hope that when the *yetzer hara* tries to influence my chassidim to sin, they will not listen to him — not because they refuse his counsel, but because they are so busy that they have no time to listen to his rantings."

(Imrei Emes)

Reb Getzel felt that it was time to begin to prepare for his final journey. He had his carriage prepared and traveled to the house of his eldest son.

When he arrived, his grandchildren surrounded him and greeted him affectionately. He tenderly kissed each one before going inside to speak to their father.

With only the briefest of greetings, Reb Getzel said to his son, "My dear boy, I have come to ask what you plan to do on my soul's behalf when you return from my funeral."

The son was shocked by his father's talk of his funeral, and he tried to demur, assuring his father that he had many more years to enjoy in this world.

"Don't waste my time," Reb Getzel insisted calmly. "I plan to visit your two brothers as well."

Seeing that his father was serious, the son considered the various possibilities for honoring those who are deceased. After some thought, he told Reb Getzel that he would build a shul bearing his father's name. In addition, on his yahrtzeit, *he would donate a Torah scroll in his father's memory. He would also fund a* Tehillim *group, the largest in the land, and name it "Chevras Getzel."*

"I will also pay numerous righteous Torah scholars to pray for your soul each year," the son concluded. "Then I will collect their original Torah thoughts and publish them to commemorate your name."

"Excellent!" Reb Getzel declared, delighted with his son's ideas. He left the house and traveled to the home of his second son to discuss the topic further.

His second son listened to his father's account of his elder brother's suggestions and dismissed them as unexceptional. "It would be better to establish a yeshivah," he declared. "We will call it 'Zichron Getzel.' Every book in the yeshivah will include an inscription that all Torah studied with this sefer will be in the merit of the soul of Getzel, son of Feivel."

Reb Getzel, feeling very satisfied, departed from his second son and made his way to the home of his youngest child. This son was said to be blessed with both his father's insight and his mother's sharpness, and Reb Getzel couldn't wait to hear his ideas.

As soon as the son heard why his father had come, he left the room briefly, returning after a short time with a package of candles.

"Father, please accompany me to a place outside the city," he requested. "First-hand experience is superior to word of mouth." He advised his father to put some candles into his pocket, for the place they were going to visit would be very dark.

Reb Getzel, impatient, did not want to take the time to pack candles. "We will use yours," he muttered hurriedly, and father and son set off.

After some travel, Reb Getzel's son indicated that they had arrived at their destination. The two men alighted from the carriage, and Reb Getzel followed his son off the road and through a forest, until they reached the entrance to a cave.

It took only a few steps into the cave before they were engulfed by darkness. The son lit a candle and led his father deeper inside. Reb Getzel's curiosity grew from moment to moment. How much longer would they continue?

Twenty minutes later, the candle flickered and went out.

"Light another candle," Reb Getzel told his son nervously.

"I have none," the son replied. "Please, Father, light the candles that are in your pocket."

In a trembling voice, Reb Getzel protested, "I did not bring the candles. I relied on you."

"My honored father," the son said gently, "that is exactly what I wished to show you. You should not rely on anyone else. As long as you live, you should be collecting mitzvos for the elevation of your own soul. Study as much Mishnah and Talmud as you possibly can, and do as many mitzvos as time allows. You have discovered what your loved ones will do for the sake of your soul, but it is far more valuable to ask yourself, 'What am I doing for the elevation of my soul?' "

(*Chaim She'yesh Bahem*, pages 109–112)

Rav Mordechai Leib Ha'kohein Kaminski's motto was, "What must be completed tomorrow should be accomplished yesterday." He lived in a small attic furnished with a little table, a kerosene stove with one burner, and a kettle; he used these simple furnishings to make the most of every minute.

Each night, before going to sleep, he filled the stove with just enough kerosene to heat the kettle. He prepared the wick for a medium flame, and filled the kettle with enough water for a single cup of tea. When he arose at midnight, he lit the stove and then recited several chapters of Tehillim. *After completing a certain number, he knew the water had boiled. With his tea prepared, he proceeded to his regimen of Torah study and prayer, without wasting a single moment.*

(*Sippurim Yerushalayim*, pages 82–83)

Food For Thought

Mitzvos requires *zerizus*; *aveiros* require laziness.

(*Ha'bayis Ha'yehudi*)

A person should rush to the *beis medrash* (*Chareidim*; *Chayei Adam*). If he hastens to a Torah lecture but does not retain what he has heard, he will still be rewarded for his alacrity. Mitzvos done with *zerizus* receive additional reward. (Rabbi Chaim Palagi, *Nefesh Ha'Chaim*, Gate 7, Chapter 29)

The moment when a mitzvah presents itself is decisive. If a person tarries, it will be difficult to step out of his comfort zone and deal with the demands of the mitzvah. But if he rises to the occasion with alacrity, the obstacles scatter and vanish. (Rav Tzadok Ha'kohein)

It is said that nothing stands in the way of desire. Desire refers to a deep-seated commitment to achieving a goal. The soul takes control over the mind and body, as the person dedicates himself towards the performance of the mitzvah.

Consider the Jews who left Egypt—they had to leave at that very moment, seizing the opportunity to depart. If a person waits, enthusiasm cools, and the mitzvah is usually lost. (Chida, *Chomas Ancha*)

Food For Thought

Repeatedly the term *remiya* is used in *Mishlei* to signify the opposite of industry. This expression usually connotes deceit but throughout *Mishlei* it appears to mean sloth, idleness, negligence, etc. And in truth, the person who does not spend his life and the spiritual and physical powers that were bestowed on him for their manifest purpose does commit deceit. He betrays the sacred charge and opportunity entrusted to him; he betrays his Maker, who grants him strength, by failing in the duty that is expected from him in return. Consequently, the very air that a lazy person breathes can be considered theft.
(Rabbi S.R. Hirsch, *From the Wisdom of Mishlei*, page 164)

Mitzvos And Matzos

All opinions concede that the trait of *zerizus* is fundamental in serving Hashem, yet this key element is presented in the Torah only in a roundabout manner. We can find a hint concealed within the command to guard the matzos (*Shemos* 12:17). In the Holy Tongue, the words *matzos* and *mitzvos* are spelled identically. Rashi, citing the *Mechilta*, explains that the command to "guard the matzos" also includes a command to "guard the mitzvos" — if the opportunity arises to perform a mitzvah, do it immediately. Just as dough must be quickly made into matzoh before it can sour and become *chometz*, so should a mitzvah be fulfilled at the earliest moment possible.

A question arises: Why doesn't the Torah clearly state that mitzvos should be performed with *zerizus*? Why hide this lesson within the laws of matzoh?

A person does not have to actively seek to turn dough into leaven; in fact, it is enough to just let the dough sit idly, and it will rise and become *chometz*. Mitzvos should be considered in the same fashion: if they are not performed with alacrity, if a person delays, then he might miss the opportunity to do the mitzvah at all. (*Nachlas Eliezer*)

There is another important lesson to be learned from the laws of matzoh. The halachic difference between *chometz* and matzoh is hardly noticeable in appearance or texture. It is the *zerizus* that separates them. A moment's delay can turn matzoh, which is fit for eating on Pesach, into *chometz*, which is forbidden to be consumed on Pesach. Mitzvos, too, can seem outwardly similar, but a mitzvah done with *zerizus* is vastly different from a mitzvah that is performed without it.

Two masmidim studied in the beis medrash of Rav Yitzchok Molcho in Salonika. One was a genius with an incredibly penetrating mind, but he was known to be quite attached to his creature comforts and was slow to extend himself for a mitzvah. The second scholar was not blessed with the first's acumen, but he was famous for his alacrity and joy in performing mitzvos as soon as the opportunity arose.

Whenever the more accomplished scholar would share his chiddushim with Rav Yitzchok, the Rav would compliment him highly. However, when the other scholar would enter the beis medrash, Rav Molcho would rise as a show of respect.

After some time, the first scholar approached Rav Yitzchok and respectfully asked for an explanation. The Rav was not obligated to stand for either of them, because his scholarship surpassed them both. But there was no doubt that he was far more accomplished than the second talmid chacham. Why, then, did the Rav stand in respect for the second scholar, but not for him?

Rav Molcho explained, "While your knowledge is greater than his, his zerizus proves that all of his learning is done for the sake of Heaven, and his study is therefore worthy of respect. Your own attitude, however, shows that you lack love of Hashem. If you would only internalize your learning, you would feel a powerful love of Hashem. The natural outgrowth of such love is zeal to do His will!"

Rav Chaim Friedlander explains that while *chometz* is the result of the natural fermentation process, matzoh is above and beyond nature, for the natural process is hindered when the baking is hastened. *Chometz* is compared to the *yetzer hara* of laziness, which convinces a person to just lie back and take it easy. The only way to "supernaturally" free ourselves from this *yetzer hara* is to perform our tasks quickly. (*Sifsei Chaim*)

If dough is prepared to use as matzoh but it is not guarded, that sluggishness results in the degradation of the dough, and it can no longer be used for the mitzvah of matzoh. Rav Hutner explains that through delay and neglect, man lowers the mitzvah from its elevated spiritual status. The Jew who fulfills a mitzvah with *zerizus* indicates that he seeks to latch onto the eternal aspects of his commitment to Hashem, for *zerizus* is the conductor to eternity. (*Divrei Torah*, Pesach 5711)

> *Many poor and lonely people would eat regularly at the table of Rav Yehoshua Leib Diskin. One of these regulars was a childless, elderly Jew.*
>
> *One day, the Rav noticed that this individual was having trouble chewing his bread. He rose and sat down next to the old man, then softened his bread and fed it to him piece by piece. When other family members wanted to take over, the Rav only smiled and replied, "It is my mitzvah and I will not relinquish it."*
>
> *Rav Yehoshua Leib absorbed this trait of seeking out and holding fast to mitzvos by observing his father, Rav Binyomin Diskin. One day, as Rav*

*Binyomin walked down the street, he noticed a por-
ter struggling with a heavy burden. He grabbed part
of the man's load and threw it over his shoulder.*

*The porter tried to stop him, without success. A
passerby rushed to relieve the Rav of the heavy sack,
but the Rav refused. "I saw the need and the mitzvah
is mine. I will not let it go." The porter continued on
his way with the Rav at his side.*

(Saraf Me'Brisk)

INSPIRATION

The proper measure of enthusiasm was demonstrated
in the ultimate place of Hashem's service — the *Beis
Ha'mikdash*. All sacrifices and ceremonies were completed
swiftly, with great zeal. (*Shabbos* 20) This fervor was
meant to serve as a prototype of the service of the Jewish
People throughout Eretz Yisroel, so they would fulfill all
mitzvos with an enthusiasm that shakes the soul awake
and fills the mind and body with life.

(Sifsei Chaim)

Begin With *Zerizus*

The *Tur* begins his commentary on *zerizus* by citing the
mishnah in *Avos* (5:23): "Rav Yehudah ben Teima said, 'Be
bold as a leopard, light as an eagle, swift as a deer, and
strong as a lion, to carry out the will of your Father in Heav-
en.'" Even when it appears that a mitzvah may be beyond
our reach, we must make the effort to start the project with
vigor and alacrity.

Rav Chaninah ben Dosah observed his neighbors bringing their pledges and donations to Yerushalayim. Although he was very poor, he too wanted to donate something. He went out to the desert and found a large stone that he cleaned, polished, and buffed to a brilliant shine. He then sought out laborers to help him transport the stone to Yerushalayim. They asked for five coins as payment, but Rav Chaninah did not have the money, so they moved on. Hashem then sent five angels in the guise of people, who agreed to carry his stone for him if he lent a hand. As soon as he laid his hand on the stone, he found himself in Yerushalayim. When he wanted to pay them, they disappeared; he searched for them but they were not to be found. He concluded that they had been angels.
(Midrash Koheles 1:1)

Rav Yosef Shlomo Kahanemen, in the name of his *rebbi* the Chofetz Chaim, would ask a few questions on this *midrash*. Why did Rav Chanina work on the stone when he knew that he could not bring it to Yerushalayim? Why did he negotiate with laborers when he had no money to pay them? Why did Hashem wait to send him angels until after the laborers abandoned him?

The lesson of this story is that we are obligated to act to the best of our ability, even if it seems that we will be unable to finish the project. Once we have begun, and we have done as much as we possibly can, then Hashem will help us finish — even if it requires miraculous intervention. (*Ha'rav Mi'Ponovezh*, Part II, page 269)

Yisroel Meir Kagan was only eleven years old when his father died. His widowed mother could barely support them both and was not able to hire someone to study Torah with him.

The young boy did not let that stand in his way. He said to himself, "I know fifty pages of Gemara already. I will keep reviewing them until Hashem helps me find some way of learning more."

So he reviewed those same fifty pages until he knew them backwards and forwards. Occasionally, he would glance at a new page of Gemara that beckoned to him like some magical mystery, and daven that Hashem send him someone who could teach him more Gemara.

One day, Yisroel Meir decided to try to work on a new page. He figured out the first few words, and when the next words gave him trouble, he turned to Rashi for help. In this way, he soon reached the understanding that had eluded him for so long. Only then did he realize that Hashem had answered his prayers for someone to teach him the new Gemara. He had revealed to the future Chofetz Chaim that if he really tried, he could teach himself.

Zerizus was a hallmark of the Imrei Emes's life. He gave new meaning to the concept of using one's time wisely. In the course of one day, he managed to learn with his sons, sons-in-law, and his grandchildren, as well as deliver numerous shiurim. He also would record his original Torah thoughts and respond to numerous letters and telegrams.

To make the most of his time, he recorded his responses with a single letter. The letter kaf *stood for "kein" and meant yes;* lamed *stood for "lo" and meant no. The letter* mem *stood for "maskim" and signified his agreement. Beis meant "beracha" and denoted that he gave his blessings. He would wordlessly hand his son-in-law the pile of correspondence, and his son-in-law would pen the replies according to specific guidelines and send them off in the Rebbe's name.*

The Imrei Emes also received hundreds of chassidim on a regular weekday, and thousands before holidays. He would absorb the meaning of each kvittel *with a single glance and respond appropriately.*

The Rebbe was always networking with Agudas Yisroel and other charitable organizations. There was no important communal or educational initiative in which he did not play a major role. Despite his demanding schedule, he always ate and slept at regular hours, davened on time, and started each learning session punctually.

(*Rosh Golas Ariel,* pages 256–259)

INSPIRATION

Rav Moshe Chaim Luzzatto describes *zerizus* as an introduction to the mitzvos. Why *zerizus*? Rav Abba Grossbard explains, in the name of the Alter of Kelm, that an introduction is intended to introduce the concepts of a book so the reader can gain the most out of reading it. Similarly, *zerizus* is the prologue through which a person acquires the knowledge to properly approach the successful fulfillment of all the mitzvos.

When the Chofetz Chaim realized that there was a great need for a sefer summarizing day-to-day halachos, he approached several great rabbis with the suggestion that they author such a book. Each one agreed that it was necessary, but none were able to put in the time or energy to do it. So the Chofetz Chaim resolved to fill the void himself. After twenty-six years of work, he completed the Mishnah Berurah.

Rav Zerach Braverman was a disciple of the Maharil Diskin. He himself had numerous students who came from various villages and hamlets throughout Eretz Yisroel.

One Shabbos, he dreamt that one of his young students was smoking on Shabbos. He did not take the dream seriously, reminding himself that dreams are often just nonsense, but on the next Shabbos, he had the same dream. He sought out the student and said to him, "I will tell you when and where you lit a cigarette this Shabbos and last Shabbos." Then he added, "My child, I do not hold it against you. But please, tell me why you did it!"

With a pained expression, the boy replied, "My dear teacher, I will tell you the truth. I studied in a school in Rishon L'tziyon, where I was born. In this school, one of the teachers would often repeat that everyone is permitted to do what his heart desires. To this day, that thought hounds me."

Rav Zerach sighed with great anguish. "I am at fault that there is no cheder in Rishon L'tziyon," he cried out.

After Shabbos, he called a meeting with his Rebbetzin and their married children, and asked them to bring him every piece of jewelry that they owned. With the money he received from selling their jewelry, he hired a G-d-fearing rebbi and convinced him to move to Rishon L'tziyon. He then went from parent to parent, gathering boys together, and eventually founded a cheder—the first of many that Rav Zerach established.

He worked tirelessly on founding one school after another, enrolling new students and collecting funds. He would continue nonstop until he collapsed on one of the benches in a local shul. Then, after sleeping for a quarter of an hour, he would get up and continue his holy work.

(Le'hagid, Bamidbar)

One morning the Steipler hastened to arrange the funeral of his daughter's father-in-law, Rav Yitzchok Berman. When Rav Moshe Mordechai

Shulsinger opened the door and found the Steipler standing there, he stammered, "Why couldn't the Rav simply have sent someone to arrange the matter?"

But the Steipler never relegated to others what he was obligated to do himself. When someone asked him a question relating to the placement of a mezuzah, he hurried to the questioner's house so he could see the matter for himself. Even when he found it difficult to walk, he would accompany his guests, carrying his chair with him so he could lean on it until he got to his door.

One winter Friday, Rav Yitzchok Silberstein was studying with his brother-in-law, Rav Chaim Kanievsky. A man interrupted their studies with a shidduch proposal for a boy who was an orphan. He asked Rav Chaim to get involved to promote the matter.

As soon as the two finished their learning session and Rav Chaim davened Minchah, he walked to the widow's house to suggest the match. The family was astonished to see the Rav at their door with a shidduch proposal at such a late hour, but it did not even occur to Rav Chaim to postpone a mitzvah for a later time.

(Kol Be'rama, Nissan 5762)

Food For Thought

Rav Yechezkel Avramsky defined a masmid as some-one who learns sixty minutes per hour. A person who masters the character trait of zerizus can cram those sixty minutes with limitless accomplishments. He will do everything immediately: rise immediately, learn, daven, and eat immediately, and never waste his time. This elongates the daily stretch of time many times over. A person who lives for eighty years in this manner uses the time as if he lived eight hundred years.

(Rav Ben Zion Abba Shaul)

Rabbi Mordechai Dov Dubin devoted himself to the needs of the Jewish People.

One Motzaei Tisha B'Av, he concluded that it was imperative that he abort his vacation and return to Riga to take care of a crucial matter. The people staying with him wondered why he could not put off his return until the next day. They advised him to rest after the fast and leave the next morning.

Rabbi Mordechai Dov replied, "I will share a story with you. One Yom Kippur, I davened alongside Rav Chaim Ozer Grodzinsky in Vilna. On Motzaei Yom Kippur, I accompanied him home. When we arrived at his home, forty people were waiting to speak to him. Rav Chaim Ozer immediately turned his attention to his petitioners with great love and devotion, without even having a bite to eat!"

(*Uvdos Le'beis Brisk*)

A group of community activists came to the Chazon Ish for advice. With his help, they resolved to undertake certain commitments. The Chazon Ish recognized that for all their good intentions, they were likely to procrastinate instead of putting their decisions into effect.

"It was Bilaam who advised the nobles of Moav to 'stay overnight,'" he reminded them. "Worthy decisions must be implemented immediately, and not be put off for tomorrow."

(*Zachor Le'David*, page 190)

One Erev Yom Kippur, the Brisker Rav sent for Rav Moshe David Tennenbaum. He asked him to arrange a deferral for a gifted yeshivah boy who had received a draft notice by mistake.

"I'll take care of it right after Yom Kippur," Rav Tennenbaum assured him.

"No," the Brisker Rav said. "I want you to take care of this matter today."

Rav Tennenbaum, taken aback, tried to explain to the Rav that all the offices were already closed for Yom Kippur.

"I wish to make sure that the matter is successfully addressed today," the Brisker Rav insisted.

Rav Tennenbaum tried again to explain that it simply couldn't be done.

"You can say that you don't want to do it," the Brisker Rav told him, "or that it is difficult for you to see it through. But don't tell me that you can't."

When Rav Tennenbaum heard those words, he was determined to see what he could do. He called the house of one of the senior commanders responsible for conscription and asked him to put the matter right. The commander tried to defer all action until after Yom Kippur, but Rav Tennenbaum would not be deterred. He persuaded the official to go back to his office and sign the deferral, all before the onset of Yom Kippur.

When the Brisker Rav was informed of the good news, he smiled and said, "May you be blessed with the same measure of delight you have given me!"

(Tuvcha Yabiu)

Food For Thought

"Wake up, my brothers!" the teacher called. "A guest you have never seen has arrived. Once he leaves, you will never see him again."

"Who is that guest?" they asked.

Their teacher replied, "Today!"

Focusing On The Goal

Zerizus enables us to focus on one goal while putting all other thoughts aside. As soon as a person contemplates doing a mitzvah, the thought's impact in heaven nourishes numerous spiritual forces, which surround him with a heavenly light that assists him in completing the mitzvah. (*Nefesh Ha'Chaim*, Gate 1, Chapter 12) This is the reason that a diligent person can overcome all obstacles, great and small. The Divine spirit, assisted by the spiritual forces his commitment has engendered, can break through every barrier. (*Perek Teshuvah*)

The Ksav Sofer traveled frequently to Vienna to take care of communal needs. A member of his community once asked the Rav to approach a certain gentile residing in Vienna and ask that he help him with an important issue. Rav Sofer assured the man that he would do whatever was in his power to settle the matter.

While in Vienna, Rav Sofer discovered that the gentile was not yet in town and would only return on Rosh Ha'shanah. Although he was expected to return to his hometown and spend Rosh Ha'shanah with his congregation, the Ksav Sofer remained in Vienna over Rosh Ha'shanah so he could speak to the gentile. On Rosh Ha'shanah itself, he walked two hours to meet the man and speak to him!

Food For Thought

A happy spirit accompanies mitzvos done with *zerizus*.

(*Kli Yakar, Shemos* 14:4)

The Samak, Rabbi Yitzchak of Korbeil, equates *zerizus* with love. A person who loves Hashem takes immediate action to avoid sinning.

(*Sefer Mitzvos Katan*, Mitzvah 4)

Deeds done with *zerizus* have lasting power. The first two letters of *zerizus* are *zayin* and *reish*, which spells *zer*, or wreath. Our enthusiasm for mitzvos is woven into a crown for Hashem.

(*Sefas Emes, Shemos* 4:25)

A mitzvah is deficient if it lacks enthusiasm, but a person can achieve magnificent results by focusing his energy on his specific goal. Picture yourself moving with enthusiasm towards your goal, doing the mitzvos with eagerness and joy. Imagine the barriers to your achievements melting away. (*Maharal, Nesiv Ha'zerizus*)

Rabbi Eliezer, who was always the first to arrive at the house of study in the morning and the last to leave at night, noticed one morning that the garbage collectors and farm laborers had risen before him. He chastised himself, "They are getting up to work for their own personal reasons, while I rise ostensibly to serve Hashem — yet they precede me."

(*Midrash Shir Ha'shirim 1*)

The first Belzer Rebbe, known as the Sar Sha-lom, worked alongside the common laborers in the construction of the shul in Belz. When asked to ex-plain, he shared the following story:

"*Many years ago, I studied Torah in the town of Skohl with two study partners. We had been taught that if we were to study with the utmost diligence and dedication, never sleeping for one thousand nights in a row, we would merit a revelation from Eliyahu Ha'navi. The three of us were very excited at this prospect, and we resolved that we would study together for a thousand consecutive nights without sleep.*

"*Despite our initial enthusiasm, first one study partner and then another abandoned the project. Soon I was the only one fighting off sleep, night after night, more determined then ever to succeed. Sleep was my constant enemy, threatening to overcome my resolve. With my Rebbetzin's encouragement, I somehow found the strength to continue, for my de-sire to see the prophet burned in my soul.*

"*On the thousandth night, a fierce storm blew into town. It seemed that the forces of nature were conspiring to destroy all my hard-won efforts. I was shaken by the unearthly howls and piercing bolts of lightning that flashed across the sky. Still, I sat with my open sefer, determined that nothing would deter me from my goal.*

"*Suddenly, there was a loud crash of glass. The wind had blown out one of the windows of the beis* midrash, *and my candles were extinguished. This was too much for me. I had studied for a thousand nights, relentlessly pursing my goal though my strength, and I was all but exhausted—and now this! The rain and wind pelted my face through the shattered window.*

"*I strengthened myself. This was my last night, after which I could expect a visit from the Eliyahu Ha'navi himself! I could not let this storm, no matter how fierce, deprive me of my reward. I felt my way to the holy ark and slid open the carved doors. Then I wept, begging Hashem to help me through this trial. I don't know how long I stood there weeping and praying, but when I finished pouring out my yearning and frustration to the One Above, I realized that the storm had ended.*

"*I turned to look out of the shattered window and saw the moon peeking through the remaining clouds. Then something else caught my attention. There, in the darkness, I saw the figure of an old man slowly approaching the study hall, and I knew it was Eliyahu Ha'navi.*

"*We sat and studied together throughout that unforgettable night. The last part of Torah that he taught me concerned the laws of building a synagogue. This teaching is so precious to me that I would erect the entire building single-handedly, from beginning to end, if I possibly could.*

"*Alas, such a task is beyond me; this little bit is all I am able to do. But even so, it is so dear to me that my entire being is filled with indescribable joy with each brick that I supervise."*

When Rav Yitzchok Elchanan Spector was a youngster, he studied with a friend in the local beis medrash. *Together the two studied almost nonstop, forging upwards in their Torah knowledge.*

One year, when the fast of Yom Kippur had ended, Yitzchok Elchanan's friend hurried home to eat something, but quickly returned to the beis medrash *to continue their studies from where they had stopped before the fast's onset. The two boys had not agreed on any specific time for resuming their learning, but it was understood that at the first available moment, they would be back at their posts.*

He was astonished to find Yitzchok Elchanan already waiting for him. "How did you get back so quickly?" he asked, wondering how anyone could have been quicker than he.

Yitzchok Elchonon smiled knowingly. "I didn't have to hurry back — I never left. Yesterday I hid some food in a corner. I ate what I prepared and returned to my Gemara immediately."

(*Derashas Ha'maggid, Moadim III*, pages 142–143)

Rav Shach had a chavrusa, *Rav David Zimmerman, who learned with him every morning until Minchah at 1 p.m.*

It once happened that the Philadelphia Rosh Yeshivah, Rav Elye Svei, came to consult Rav Shach on a certain matter. The discussion lasted until 12:45 p.m.

As soon as Rav Svei left, Rav Shach asked, "Where is Rav Zimmerman?"

Rav Zimmerman hurried inside, but he wondered aloud, "There are only a few minutes left to Minchah. Is the Rosh Yeshivah certain that he wants to sit down and learn?"

Rabbi Shach was emphatic. "A few minutes of learning is eternity," he declared.

(*Torah Leaders*, page 9)

Rav Hirsch Michel Shapira learned constantly, studying not only during the day, but also most of the night. Immediately after Maariv, he would go to one of the Sephardic yeshivos in the Old City, stand by one the tables, and learn Shulchan Aruch, Choshen Mishpat *until it was nearly midnight. Never once in all that time did he even think of sitting down. He kept a special cane with him at night, and if he felt particularly sleepy, he would ask one of the scholars in the* beis medrash *to rap him over the fingers with it if he dozed off.*

When midnight approached, he would ask one of the scholars sitting nearby to wake him in ten minutes. Then, still standing, he would close his eyes and take a short nap. When he was awakened at midnight, he immersed himself in the mikveh, *seated* himself on the hard, cold floor, and wept for Zion and the Beis Ha'mikdash. With his mourning completed, he would return to the Shulchan Aruch. Dawn would find him still on his feet, learning with the utmost concentration. He would stop just long enough to daven Shacharis and partake of a frugal meal.

(*Men of Distinction*, page 137)

Rav Ben Zion Abba Shaul was careful not to waste a moment of precious Torah study time. One morning on his way to yeshivah, he saw a student examining a billboard poster. Rav Ben Zion cried out: "SOS! SOS!" and continued on his way.

The student ran after him and breathlessly asked, "What happened? Who needs help?"

"The entire world!" Rav Ben Zion returned. "If you don't study Torah, the world will be destroyed. If you were an ambulance driver or a paramedic, and you were summoned to save a life, would you stop to read the latest announcements? As a Torah scholar your job is far more vital, because the world is maintained only in the merit of Torah study."

(*Yated Neeman*)

Rav Moshe Aharon Levi served as shochet in the city of Lomza, at the time when the gaon Rav Yehoshua Leib Diskin was its Rav. Rav Moshe Aharon *possessed a fiery Jewish heart and a fierce commitment to Torah and Yiddishkeit, as befit a man who could trace his ancestry to one of the most prominent disciples of the Vilna Gaon.*

In secularized Lomza, Reb Moshe Aharon found himself with little means to feed his growing family. When he was offered a position as Rav and shochet *in a Jewish community of Lithuanian extraction in America, he felt as if he were forced to choose between two evils. Should he subject his family to death by starvation in Europe, or asphyxiation of the soul in America?*

He consulted Rav Yehoshua Leib, who advised him to accept the offer in America. "I am confident," the Rav told him, "that your blazing devotion to Hashem will not be extinguished, even in America!"

He left his family in Lithuania, sending them money regularly through Rav Diskin. In a short time, he established himself in Brooklyn, where he was highly respected for his Torah scholarship and well liked for his exceptional character. After a number of years, he felt that he had created an appropriately sheltered environment, and he felt comfortable in bringing his family to America.

When his daughters came of age, however, he could not find them appropriate shidduchim. *Then, one Shabbos, he overheard one daughter tell the other that it would be impossible to marry a* ben Torah *as they might have done in Lithuania. "Here in America," she said, "we will have to compromise, and find a businessman who at least knows how to learn."*

Rav Moshe Aharon's blood turned cold at these words. He said nothing on Shabbos, but right after Havdalah, he turned to his wife, Miriam, and announced, "We must pack our bags and get out of here as quickly as we can."

His devoted wife was taken aback by the intensity of his declaration. Why did they have to hurry? Who was running after them?

Rav Moshe Aharon explained that they would never merit the kind of descendants they wished as long as they remained in America. "We will go to Yerushalayim," he said. "There, we will be able to marry off our daughters to the kind of Torah scholars we desire."

They sold everything they owned, converting their possessions into gold coins as they finalized the preparations to move to Yerushalayim. Rav Moshe Aharon's congregation was devastated at his imminent departure, and they did everything they could to prevent it. In the end, the family was forced to creep out of the city in the middle of the night.

When they arrived in Yerushalayim, Reb Moshe Aharon made his way to the house of his beloved Rav, the Maharil Diskin. The Rebbetzin opened the door and shouted in joy to her husband, "Your blessing has come true! Reb Moshe Aharon came back from America with his family, and they have remained G-d-fearing."

Rav Yehoshua Leib received Rav Moshe Aharon with great joy and blessed him that he should obtain sons-in-laws that were both great scholars and pious individuals.

This blessing was soon fulfilled. Reb Eliyahu Rohm, the most desirable catch in Yerushalayim, was besieged with marriage proposals. The gaon Rav Shmuel Salant, acting as his advisor, selected Rav Moshe Aharon's daughter for the shidduch. Rav Shmuel assured Rav Moshe Aharon that this young man would one day be a great Torah scholar, certain to grace the beis din of Yerushalayim. Rav Moshe Aharon did not hesitate and rushed to finalize the shidduch, promising a few years of total support so Reb Eliyahu could continue his studies without distractions.

It was only by acting without delay, to preserve the family's spirituality, that Rav Moshe Aharon merited such a distinguished son-in-law.

(Borchi Nafshi, Shemos, pages 311–314)

The Rav of a certain Polish city was speaking to the one of the city's most respected citizens when he heard the terrible news: one of the factories in the city, owned by a Jew, was operating on Shabbos.

The Rav turned to the man at his side and asked him to escort him to the factory owner's office to defend the honor of Shabbos. The presence of such a prominent citizen, the Rav felt, would surely have a major impact on the businessman.

The man immediately agreed, but asked the Rav to wait for just a few moments while he changed. He gestured at his attire: he was wearing slippers, not shoes, and his shirt had just been spattered with mud.

"I will go home, change my shirt, and don my shoes," he said. "Then I will go with the Rav."

"We cannot wait," the Rav said firmly. "If we don't go immediately, the yetzer hara will erode our determination to defend the honor of Shabbos." With a smile, he added, "Don't worry. No one will notice your slippers."

The two of them made their way to the office of the errant businessman. The owner, unsuspecting, greeted them warmly. But when the Rav related why they had come, he was shocked and horrified—the factory had been opened on Shabbos without his authorization. He promised that he would immediately take steps to ensure that all work on Shabbos would come to a halt, and that no one would ever be able to act behind his back again.

"There's just one thing I don't understand," the factory owner said as he escorted his prominent guests out of the office. "How did the Rav know that I am about to leave on an extended business trip? If the Rav had come just a few minutes later, I would have already left!"

The Rav hadn't known, of course, but the man who had accompanied him was awed by this manifest proof of the necessity of zerizus in a mitzvah. If they had delayed their errand, even for the few minutes to change his shirt and shoes, they would have

missed the manufacturer. They would most likely
have met only with resistance from his assistants,
and the chillul Shabbos *would have persisted until the*
businessman's return. Thanks to the Rav's insistence
on alacrity, the sanctity of Shabbos was preserved.
                    (*Borchi Nafshi, Bereishis*, pages 144–146)

When an opportunity to perform a mitzvah arises, we
should pursue it immediately. We are told in *Avos* to run for
a mitzvah, because if we don't, it may never become a reality.
(Rav Yisroel Salanter)

> *Rav Yisroel Salanter once gave Rav Simcha Zis-*
> *sel of Kelm a letter to mail. Rav Simcha Zissel, aware*
> *of the contents of the letter, felt sure that there was*
> *no need to rush to accomplish the task.*
>
> *A short time later, during the course of a de-*
> *rashah, Rav Yisroel noted that a person can lose his*
> *portion in the World to Come if he neglects doing*
> *something that requires alacrity. Rav Simcha Zissel*
> *was convinced that Rav Yisroel knew of his decision*
> *to put off mailing the letter through* ruach ha'kodesh.

> *The Chofetz Chaim was always quick to take ac-*
> *tion. Whenever he had an idea that might benefit*
> *someone, he always acted on it immediately.*
>
> *One day, he asked his son-in-law Rav Tzvi to*
> *translate his book,* Geder Olam, *into Yiddish. Later*
> *that same afternoon, he asked Rav Tzvi if someone*
> *had begun working on the translation. The next*

morning, when he discovered that no action had been taken, he began translating the work himself.

When Yaakov was on his way to Lavan's house, he realized that he had missed a spiritually significant opportunity. He immediately turned back towards Eretz Yisroel, even though he was nearly at his destination. Because he proved his determination to return with alacrity, Hashem aided him by enabling him to reach Har Ha'moriah quickly.

> *Rav Nosson Wachtfogel required the assistance of a certain person in a matter of great importance. The* Mashgiach *insisted on personally calling the man, but he was not at home. In his desire to track the man down, Rav Nosson called both his parents and in-laws. When neither of them knew where he was, he asked for the names of friends and tried calling them as well. They, too, could not help locate the man in question.*
>
> *Those who were assisting him felt they had extended every possible effort. What else could they do? But the* Mashgiach *refused to abandon the project. He had no further suggestions, but he knew they had to keep trying!*
>
> *Just then, the phone rang — and it was the person that the* Mashgiach *was seeking.*
>
> *After speaking to him, the* Mashgiach *hung up the phone and turned to the others in the room. "Do you see?" he declared. "When you try and don't give up, Hashem sends help from heaven."*
>
> (*Yated Neeman*, 8 Kislev 5769)

Objects of little worth are generally easily acquired, while one must work hard to obtain something very precious. That is why strenuous labor is needed to dwell in the holy presence of Hashem. It takes great wisdom to sidestep the *yetzer hara* and prevent his involvement in our deeds as he seeks to prevent us from doing mitzvos. (*Madreigos Ha'adam*) "The lazy man is wiser in his own eyes than seven Sages," says Shlomo Ha'melech (*Mishlei* 26:16). A person's laziness does not allow him to consider the words of those who rebuke him. He thinks that everyone else is mistaken and he alone is wise.

By utilizing *zerizus*, and engaging in acts that may be demanding, great things can be accomplished for oneself and for the benefit of the Jewish nation. Any act of delay usually results in further deferment, and might spell the end of a great endeavor.

INSPIRATION

"When something needed to be done, I never gave any thought as to whether I was able to do it or not. If I was certain that it was necessary, I would find a way to get it done."

(Alter of Novardok)

Enthusiasm And Deliberation

Zerizus is the force that enables us to pursue spirituality. A weakness of will and effort is a major obstacle to spiritual ascent, for our materialistic needs distract us from our ultimate goal. Only deliberation, coupled with enthusiasm, can result in excellence.

However, enthusiasm alone is not enough! First we must consider the best way to proceed, and then take action, quickly utilizing the combined strength and efforts of all the powers of our body and soul. (*Malbim*) Enthusiasm without deliberation is like a silver vessel that is adulterated by inferior metals, which is removed from the forge before it can be rid of its impurities. Zeal must be kept under control, or it can lead to negative practices such as self-indulgence. (*Toras Avos*)

INSPIRATION

There were many reasons why Boaz might have chosen to procrastinate about marrying Rus. He was the leader of the generation (*Rus Rabbah, Parshah* 5); he was very old (*Rus Rabbah, Parshah* 6); and the matter was complicated. Nevertheless, Boaz undertook the redemption of Rus with great speed. He met with the closer relative in the presence of the Sanhedrin, redeemed the fields that blocked their union, and took Rus as his wife — all in one day. When Hashem saw his determination, He arranged that no obstacles be placed in Boaz's way and enabled Rus to conceive immediately. (*Sifsei Chaim*)

The Chofetz Chaim viewed Boaz as the quintessential *zariz*. He first deliberated as to how to proceed, then moved swiftly to resolve the matter.

(*Dugmah Mi'sichos Avi*, page 90)

Anticipate the mitzvos you will be doing and plan ahead. Work on overcoming your tendency to laziness so all your senses are on the alert. Be prepared to take action — but only after deliberation. Thus you will be able to eliminate laziness and become diligent. (*Nesivos Ha'osher*)

"And you will see that the man whose soul burns in the service of his Creator will certainly not be lazy about fulfilling His commandments. Instead, his movements will be as rapid as the quick motion of fire. For he will not rest, and he will not be still, until he has completed the task to perfection." (*Mesilas Yesharim, Zerizus*)

As you perform the mitzvah, move quickly — but your mind should be relaxed and focused, like an ambulance driver hurrying to the hospital. It is true that he must hurry, but he also has to be careful to avoid an accident! (Rav Ben Zion Abba Shaul)

Completing The Deed

Zerizus is not just doing a mitzvah at the first opportunity, but also seeing it through to its completion. Lazy people have a difficult time completing anything. (*Mesilas Yesharim*, Chapter 7) Even after we begin performing a mitzvah, the *yetzer hara* still tries to stop us by numbing our minds with a sense of satisfaction — so we forget that we must conclude what we have started.

Shlomo Ha'melech advises us in *Mishlei* that we observe the ant and become wise. The Chida asks why the verse doesn't recommend that we observe the ant and become energetic. He explains that it is wise to extrapolate from the ant's steadfast enthusiasm and apply it to our own commitment to Torah and mitzvos.

One reason for our habitual sluggishness is our nature: we were formed out of earth, so we are weighed down by our earthy tendencies. (Rav Samson Raphael Hirsch, *Bereishis* 1:26) A person must be "bold as a leopard," with the ability to make the commitment to begin a project. He must also be "light as an eagle," and rise above any difficulties he encounters. An eagle is a heavy bird that relies on his powerful wings to soar above all threats. We, too, have the ability to uplift our onerous tendencies by using our wings of joy. (Rav Chaim Vital)

The *mishnah* from *Pirkei Avos* continues, telling a person to be "swift as a deer" by sustaining the passion necessary to persist toward a goal, thus translating plans into reality; and to be "strong as a lion," to make it possible to complete a project and bring his plans to fruition (*Alei Shur*, Vol. II). Without perseverance, even the most enthusiastic beginning can end in failure. A person without determination to continue is likely to quit before accomplishing his goals. Perseverance is the quality that enables a person to overcome the inevitable obstacles and challenges that block his way. Forging ahead, over, or around those obstacles strengthens his ability to succeed.

> *There was a man who never missed a day of his Daf Yomi shiur. Now his first son was getting married. How could he manage to attend the wedding and his* shiur *at the same time? After much thought, he came up with an ingenious idea. He arranged for the* shiur *to take place in a specially designated room at the wedding hall!*
>
> *Right after the* chuppah, *when his presence was not required, the father of the* chassan *slipped away*

from the crowd, went into the special room, and joined the others for their daily shiur. *His questions and comments that evening indicated an even greater comprehension than usual — undoubtedly inspired by his affection for his learning and his devotion to the goal of mastering* Shas.

(*Aleinu Le'shabeiach*, pages 215–216)

INSPIRATION

King Hoshea ben Elah is praised for removing the guards Yeravam had posted to prevent the Jews from visiting the *Beis Ha'mikdash*. King Hoshea announced that all who wished to go up to Yerushalayim were welcome to do so. However, because he did not make it an obligation, the value of his deed was diminished. The Ten Tribes were eventually exiled because they did not take advantage of the renewed access to Yerushalayim, and King Hoshea was exiled because he did not compel them to go to Yerushalayim. (*Chareidim*) King Hoshea angered Hashem because he began a mitzvah but did not complete it.

Before Yosef's passing, he asked that his brothers take his bones up to Eretz Yisroel (*Bereishis* 50:25). While the Jews were busy gathering their new wealth in anticipation of leaving Egypt, Moshe Rabbeinu was busy trying to recover Yosef's bones (*Shemos* 13:19; *Sotah* 13a).

However, at the actual burial of Yosef in Shechem, the *pasuk* testifies, "And the bones of Yosef, which the children of Yisroel brought up from Mitzrayim, they buried in Shechem."

Why isn't Moshe Rabbeinu credited with his burial? After all, it was only due to his determined effort that the bones were recovered and removed from Mitzrayim! Both *Metzudas David* and *Radak* explain that because the Jewish People completed the task, they are given credit for the entire mitzvah.

> *The great* mekubal, *Rav Chaim Shaul Ha'kohein Doueck, composed a* sefer *entitled* Eifah Sheleimah. *Since he lost his vision at the age of forty, two of his students helped him prepare the manuscript for publication. The two disciples divided the job, one working in the mornings and the other in the afternoons.*
>
> *It is interesting to note that at the end of the book, the author extends his thanks and blessings to only one of his students: the Kaf Ha'Chaim. The second collaborator, Rav Yehudah Petayah, took ill and had to return to Baghdad before the* sefer *was completed. With no ill intent, the mitzvah was attributed to the one who finished it.*
>
> *(Bereishis Rabbah 85:4; Ascending the Path, pages 78–79)*

INSPIRATION

When David Ha'melech heard that his fourth son Adoniya had attempted to seize power, David immediately sent for his son Shlomo. He ordered his ministers to take Shlomo to the Gichon River, the traditional place for anointing a new monarch, and publicly coronate him as the next king. As soon as the anointment took place, the rebellion was over.

Rav Moshe Chaim Luzatto wonders why David rushed to appoint Shlomo. After all, it had been prophesized that Shlomo would rule after him. The *Mesilas Yesharim* concludes, "Many obstacles can arise from here to the Gichon River." David recognized that if he waited to do things in the usual manner, new obstructions and complications could arise at every step of the way, which might derail the entire operation. To avoid any interference, David ordered the coronation to take place immediately.

(*I Melachim* 1:38; *Mesilas Yesharim*, Chapters 6–7)

Laziness Defined

A lazy person is one whose soul-powers are slumbering. He gets up at a late hour, never prepares for anything in advance, and is never on time for appointments. He does not complete his tasks; he promises a lot, but actually accomplishes very little.

He has all kinds of excuses for his behavior. He will assert that a person with a fired-up temperament is sure to develop high blood pressure, ulcers, and other serious life-threatening conditions. He is convinced that his languid style represents the best approach to life. In reality, however, he is most unfortunate. A person who is not enthusiastic about the performance of mitzvos and does not undertake spiritual commitments will find himself doomed to failure. (Rav Chaim Friedlander)

The Jewish People acknowledged their servitude to Hashem. A person can't be a part-time servant! By definition, a servant is someone who is totally subservient to his master. This obligation includes fulfilling our duty with alacrity, getting up on time, praying on time, and fulfilling all our duties with devotion and fervor.

The Imrei Emes's first act as Rebbe was to reinstate davening in their halachically defined times. Until his reign, the chassidim of Gur had followed the custom of the chassidim of Kotzk, making extensive spiritual preparations before their morning prayers and beginning Shacharis late.

The Rebbe's innovation was not received enthusiastically by the older generation, who remembered things as they had been in the days of the Sefas Emes and the Chiddushei Ha'rim. But one of these respected elder chassidim, Rav Avrohom of Purisov, advised the chassidim of Gur to follow the new ruling of their young Rebbe.

"But why innovate?" they asked him.

"Once upon a time," said Rav Avrohom, "there was a man who enjoyed his wife's cooking so much that he was prepared to wait for hours until his favorite delicacies were ready to be served. One day, after waiting patiently as usual, he took his place at the table, only to discover that he was being served lukewarm hash.

" 'What happened here?' he complained 'When I knew that you were going to give me a delicious dinner, it was worth waiting. But if this is what I am going to be served, why should the preparation take so long?'

"It is the same with us," concluded Rav Avrohom. "In the good old days, when our davening was worthy

of the name, lengthy preparations were needed and
justified. But with the humdrum type of davening that
we serve up nowadays, why should there be lengthy
preparations?"

(*Chassidim Mesaprim*)

In our day-to-day working lives, a person cannot simply decide that he is unavailable at certain times. What would happen if a bus driver decided to change his route to a more convenient one, or if a mailman felt it would be easier to distribute the mail in middle of the night? They would surely be relieved of their positions immediately! We, too, cannot do things only the way we wish to or when we feel like it, but when and how they must be done.

If we put off a mitzvah, or postpone a learning session, there is no guarantee that we will ever undertake this mitzvah. Even if you find the time to learn later, it is impossible to learn Torah properly if you do not take advantage of every available minute.

A lazy person lives a chaotic life at every level, and is incapable of even hearing those who offer him sound advice that can change his life. (Rav Ben Zion Abba Shaul, *Ohr Le'tziyon*)

An American Rav who moved to Bnai Brak told Rav Chaim Kanievsky the following story:

One of the regulars in his shul would always come
to davening ten minutes late. No matter how many
times the Rav reproved him for his laziness, the man
would reply, "What difference does ten minutes

make? At least I make it to most of davening."

One day, the man arrived on time. The Rav praised his promptness after davening and asked what had inspired the change.

"Hashem showed me, in no uncertain terms, how important ten minutes can be," the man replied.

The Rav asked him to elaborate. The man, a wealthy factory owner, explained that his plant had been destroyed by fire the day before, causing massive losses.

The shocked Rav expressed his sympathy for the man's financial loss. "But what does that have to do with davening on time?" he asked.

"As soon as the fire was discovered," the factory owner said, "we called the fire department. It took ten minutes from the time we called until the fire engines came. In that time, the fire spread from one end of the factory to the other.

"When the fire engines finally arrived, I asked why it had taken so long. The chief said to me, 'What difference does ten minutes make? The important thing is that we are here now!'

"When I heard that answer, my blood froze. It was spine-chilling how those words mirrored my responses to you over the years, when you tried to encourage me to come daven on time.

"Suddenly, the significance of ten minutes was all too clear. Then and there, I resolved to come to shul on time."

(*Borchi Nafshi*, pages 446–448)

Food For Thought

Rav Nosson Wachtfogel considered life to be a sacred mission. A loyal officer in Hashem's army is on the battlefield every day of his life. The Mashgiach felt that one should never take his mind off his mission.

He often said, "'Taking it easy' is a *treif* term, symptomatic of an American malady."

(*Torah Leaders*)

Serving Hashem is an ongoing commitment that never goes on vacation.

A lazy person will get absolutely nowhere. He becomes easily discouraged and cannot readily deal with obstacles. When our resources are not working harmoniously together towards a common goal, they must be prodded awake and forced to work. (Piaseczne Rebbe)

Food For Thought

The *yetzer hara* makes use of our laziness to his full advantage. A person might claim that he can't eat *Melaveh Malkah* because he is too full, but it is more likely that he simply can't be bothered. If he would start eating, he would see that it is manageable.

Another person may sleep a lot, claiming that he requires more sleep than other people. It is often possible to sleep less, but laziness prevents the person from making the effort.

The lazy person might daven at home during a snowfall, excusing his behavior by recalling the story he heard about a person who slipped on the snow and broke his leg.

The lazy person will surely not make any effort to bring a poor man money if it is hot or cold outside. (*Ohr Le'tziyon, Atzlus*)

Regarding the practice of *bein ha'zemanim*, Chacham Ben Zion Abba Shaul commented, "I don't understand the concept. The words don't even make sense: There is no 'time in between time.' If you can actually find 'time in between time,' that is when you can take off from learning.

Lack of purpose can be equally destructive in the realm of thought. If a person's mind is empty of resolve, the *yetzer hara* seizes the opportunity to fill his mind with negative imagery. This disastrous preoccupation occurs not only during the day, but also continues at night in dreams. Only a person focused on the particulars of his aspirations can avoid this negative trend. (Rav Chaim Friedlander)

The book of *Mishlei* is full of descriptions of the lazy individual. Many verses detail the unreliability of a lazy human being who cannot be relied on to support his family. (*Mishlei* 10:26; 11:29) A lazy person constantly sees obstacles in his way. (*Mishlei* 15:19) He has a whole repertoire of explanations for not taking action. It is too cold, or too hot; he doesn't feel well, or his head hurts (*Mesilas Yesharim*, Chapter 9). He prefers eating and sleeping to more productive work (*Mishlei* 19:15, 19:24). Even when he is starving, he will find it difficult to overcome his laziness and toil in a meaningful way. (Ralbag, ibid)

> *The Chazon Ish once asked a student to travel to Yerushalayim from Bnai Brak to help a certain person.*
>
> *"I have a wedding in Yerushalayim tomorrow," the student replied. "I will take care of the favor then."*
>
> *The Chazon Ish told him, "I can't understand you! When a favor is required, one must hurry to do it. If you wish to go to a wedding in Yerushalayim tomorrow, then tomorrow you can go again."*
>
> (Maaseh Ish)

Eliminating Laziness

Many people do not recognize the consequences of the failure of commitment. The negative effects of a weakness in will and effort do not manifest themselves immediately, because there is no visible act — just a lack of action.

> *Rav Nosson Wachtfogel once commented, "It is truly a wonder that people are not embarrassed to come late to davening. Human nature dictates that most people will do anything to avoid publicly displaying their shortcomings. But when it comes to davening, people come to shul late and do not seem*

even slightly embarrassed! It must be that they do not view laziness as a real shortcoming."

Food For Thought

Outwardly, the deliberate person and the lazy person may seem very much alike, since their actions are slow and often delayed. But there is a significant difference. The deliberate person pauses, considering the best course of action. The lazy person does not take the trouble to consider, but simply procrastinates until there is nothing to do but to act.

(Kotzker Rebbe)

The Ramchal observes that a person's desire to take it easy and indulge himself prevent him from embracing the character trait of *zerizus*. (*Mesilas Yesharim*, Chapter 9) *Atzlus*, or laziness, is the negative attitude towards work that causes negligence, half-heartedness, and poor results.

It is important to explore and determine devices and strategies that will help you uproot laziness. Think of laziness as a disease of the soul that demands that you serve as your own doctor, seeking a cure. Everything in this world is acquired through labor. We need to acquire an appreciation for life and its unlimited possibilities — in particular, the eternal rewards associated with keeping mitzvos. Even if you don't feel enthusiastic about a mitzvah, behave as if you do and actively run to fulfill it.

One first step towards mastering *zerizus* might be speaking enthusiastically about certain goals. "A tree in the darkness must be kicked until the light penetrates" (*Zohar*, quoted by the *Tanya*). You must kick yourself and force yourself to serve Hashem.

Promote your own enthusiasm: "When will I get a chance to fulfill this mitzvah? I will be so happy when this mitzvah comes my way." Argue with the *yetzer hara*: "You will not dissuade me from serving Hashem." Imitate the tone of voice and facial expressions of those people you know who are good at getting things done. Try to follow their examples as best as you can.

* * *

EXERCISE

For the next two weeks, on a daily basis, hurry to accomplish one thing that you might not have done in the past at all.

* * *

Rav Yechezkel Levenstein toiled to completely uproot his tendency to laziness. Even in his old age, when walking was difficult, he always retrieved a sefer *he wanted himself, rather than ask someone to get it for him. All his life, he served Hashem like a soldier on the battlefront, never forgetting that he was engaged in an ongoing campaign. He never leaned back comfortably in his chair; he always sat upright at the edge of the seat, whether he was home or in a bus or taxi. He maintained this custom even in his last days.*

(Mofes Ha'dor)

Rav Shalom Schwadron spent half a year in close contact with Rav Eliyahu Lopian. He observed that Rav Lopian always rose at a very early hour.

When Rav Shalom asked about this, Rav Lopian explained, "After 120 years, when I arrive in the World to Come, they will go through the entire Shulchan Aruch, *paragraph by paragraph, and ask me if I fulfilled my obligations. Presumably, the inquiry will follow the order of the text. Well, the first paragraph of the* Shulchan Aruch *declares, 'One should strengthen oneself like a lion to get up in the morning to serve one's Creator.' How will it look if I have not fulfilled the very first clause? If I rise early, at least I will receive a good grade on the first obligation!"*

(*Sheal Avicha Ve'yagedcha*, Part III, page 89)

The Steipler said that he did not understand how people could sleep late in the mornings, relying on the authorities that permit saying *Kriyas Shema* at a later hour. After all, those who ignore the time limit set by the Magen Avrohom might be transgressing a Torah obligation! At Lederman's Shul, where he regularly davened, he would always encourage the *chazan* to hurry, for fear that he would miss the earliest time for saying *Shema*. (*Toldos Yaakov*, pages 204–205)

The Klausenberger Rebbe never really went to bed.

One witness describes his nightly ritual: "I was only a boy when the Rebbe arrived in Klausenberg. I had heard unbelievable stories about his activities, and I was determined to follow him and scrutinize his deeds. One night, I hid in an unobtrusive corner of the beis medrash *so I could observe him in action.*

"The beis medrash *slowly emptied. He sat in his place and learned aloud, hour after hour. Well after midnight, he got up and recited the* Shema, *taking nearly an hour. Then he put two chairs together near the central stove and took a short nap. He woke up after a short time and began to passionately recite the morning* berachos.*"*

(*Lapid Eish*, page 113)

Food For Thought

One of the young yeshivah boys told the Sefas Emes of Gur that he found it very difficult to get up in time in the morning.

The Rebbe responded, "Each morning, we say, 'These are the things, the fruits of which a man enjoys in this world ... timely attendance at the house of study, morning and evening...' Consider the words of the mishnah. What does attendance in the evening have to do with getting up in the morning? It indicates that a man who goes to bed early can also get up in good time!"

(*Men of Distinction*, page 133)

Zerizus is so important that the Tur begins his *sefer* with the quote from *Pirkei Avos* (5:23), "Yehudah ben Teima says, 'Be bold as a leopard, light as an eagle, swift as a deer, and strong as a lion, to carry out the will of your Father in Heaven.'" The *Mesilas Yesharim* says in the chapter on *zerizus* that the lazy person does not do evil; rather, evil overtakes him because he does nothing to stop it.

Human beings are naturally lazy. There is no shortage of excellent excuses for not doing something, and most of us know them by heart. Overcoming that tendency demonstrates our love for Hashem. We must never put off a spiritual pursuit for tomorrow in the assumption that we will then have time; we might find ourselves as busy tomorrow as we are today. The spiritual progress we could have experienced today, once lost, is irretrievable. We must completely embrace each mitzvah immediately, for fear that we will not be able to complete it. (*Madreigas Ha'adam*)

When duty called, Rav Yosef Yoizel Hurwitz was suddenly transformed into a youngster. During those days of uncertainty and upheaval leading up to World War I, he traveled to distant locations without a second thought, and after each journey he literally fell into his bed from exhaustion.

He was traveling almost constantly. While recuperating from one pressing mission he would receive a telegram about another one that was just as urgent. He would then promptly set off again for three straight days of travel. He once spent Rosh Ha'shanah in Kiev, Shabbos Teshuvah in Charkov, and Yom Kippur in Hummel. He didn't worry about his family, and he wasn't concerned about his safety. In his view, he was merely a faithful servant of his

Creator, and his assignment was to ensure that Torah would not be forgotten by the Jewish People.

The trips were also full of hardship. Often left with no other choice, he would travel in the ordinary coaches of the trains. The cars were so packed that whoever was sitting couldn't get up, and whoever was standing couldn't sit down—like the plague of darkness in Egypt. It was a great miracle just to remain in the car and not be pushed out the window.

Once he went to Berditchev to encourage the students in the yeshivah there. When he arrived, the city was under siege. Shells were flying everywhere, and the enemy forces were invading and preparing to unleash a pogrom on the hapless Jewish residents. The shocked inhabitants asked the venerable Rav Yosef Yoizel why he had risked his life to come at so dangerous a time. He answered that it was his duty to strengthen the spirit of the students in the yeshivah. On hearing his reply, they wonderingly inquired, "Is now the time to worry about the morale of the yeshivah students!?" He unhesitatingly answered, "I am fighting Hashem's battles. The Torah is dying out and being forgotten. This is an emergency, and drastic measures are called for. If I don't help strengthen the yeshivos and ensure that their doors remain open, what will become of the Torah?"

———————

A young man asked Rav Yosef Chaim Sonnenfeld to speak to Rav Mordechai Leib Rubin, the head of the beis din, *on his behalf. That night it snowed heavily, and Yerushalayim woke up to a blanket of snow. Standing at his window, the young man was horrified to see Rav Yosef Chaim Sonnenfeld trudging through the snowdrifts. He ran out and asked the Rav where he was going. When he discovered that he was headed to Rabbi Rubin's house, he tearfully begged Rav Sonnenfeld to return home.*

Rav Sonnenfeld replied, "Do you think that a Jew with a white beard should not bother to fulfill a mitzvah? Doesn't it say that when a mitzvah comes your way, you should act immediately so you don't lose the opportunity? Even in the snow...."

(Ha'ish Al Ha'chomah)

The Chazon Ish once sent a family member on a mission to bring some money to a needy individual. When he saw that the relative did not leave immediately to perform the task, he told him firmly, "A person must always react to such needs as if he has come face-to-face with a conflagration. It must be done immediately."

One of the Chazon Ish's relatives received a message to come to his house immediately. When he entered, the Chazon Ish said, "I have heard that in a certain Talmud Torah, they have begun teaching English. Because I live nearby, I must take action to stop it." He asked the relative to write a letter to his father-in-law, Rav Moshe Blau, to have the subject removed from the curriculum.

It was late Friday afternoon, and the young man had not yet completed his Shabbos preparations. He asked the Chazon Ish to permit him to write the letter after Shabbos.

The Chazon Ish replied, "I am afraid to delay this matter."

The young man begged him to reconsider, and the Chazon Ish agreed—provided that he would daven Minchah Shabbos afternoon in his house, and sit down to write the letter under his supervision right after Havdalah.

By the time they concluded their conversation, it was so late that the relative deposited his muktzeh *objects with the Chazon Ish so he would not be left carrying them at the onset of Shabbos. He returned the next day as agreed, and wrote the letter in the Chazon Ish's presence. On Sunday, Rav Moshe Blau came to Bnai Brak and took care of the matter.*

(*Peer Ha'dor*, Part Four)

One Friday, about half an hour before Shabbos, Rav Menachem Porush received a message asking that he come to the Brisker Rav's house immediately.

He later related, "When I arrived, he asked me to sit down and write a letter to a wealthy man, requesting his assistance for a poor family who badly needed financial help. I could not help but ask, 'Rebbi, please explain to me why I should write this letter now, right before the zeman. *It is clear that we cannot post the letter — the post office is already closed. Why couldn't it wait until after Shabbos?'*

"The Brisker Rav looked at me with wonder and said, 'Reb Menachem, how can I be sure that I will live until tomorrow? Anything that can be done immediately should not be delayed.' Then he added, 'I have been taught by my father that one should smash walls to smithereens, if necessary, to complete a favor for someone.'"

(*Uvdos Ve'hanhagos le'beis Brisk*)

INSPIRATION

"I, Bachya son of Asher, determined that all is vanity. I saw that only wisdom had merit. I established that time is like a treacherous stream and trembled in panic.

"I then removed my garment of laziness and donned my garment of zealousness. It was a time to do for Hashem, and so I ran like a deer for His name's sake ... to write a commentary on the Torah."

(Rabbeinu Bachya, Introduction to *Chovos Ha'levavos*)

Imagine that you had access to a treasure for a limited time. You would not dawdle or procrastinate! You would rush to take as much as you can, for as long as you could. This should be our attitude towards the value of every moment of fulfilling mitzvos. (Chofetz Chaim)

Do not put off doing a mitzvah. When the alarm clock tells you that it's time to get up and begin the day, start right away! The snooze button can be the *yetzer hara*'s influence, tempting you into laziness. Do you do your work around the house before reaching for the phone to shmooze with a friend? When you see someone who needs help, do you run to help him? Do you make your *brachos* as soon as you finish eating, or do you wait? Do you come to davening on time? If you focus on a specific goal with enthusiasm, pushing aside extraneous thoughts and filling yourself with vigor, you will succeed. (*Orchos Tzaddikim*)

Rav Yehudah Zev Segal spared no effort to fulfill a mitzvah. Once, cloudy weather made it impossible to recite Kiddush Levanah. *As the time approached after which the mitzvah could not be performed, someone offered to drive Rav Segal around to search for a spot where the moon was visible. After a long time their search was successful and with great excitement they performed the mitzvah.*

INSPIRATION

"I passed by the field of a lazy man, and by the vineyard of a man lacking a [self-disciplining] heart."

(*Mishlei* 24:30)

A lazy person is called a *chaser lev*, one who lacks self-discipline. He lets things slide and doesn't grow from his experiences. A lazy person doesn't care to get at the truth. Lessons that are learned must be applied, and that would require an energetic commitment that is beyond him.

A person who is not lazy is not content with relying on

others; he checks out the vineyard himself. Once there, he does not just take a casual look, but deliberates and processes the lessons that can be gleaned from the incident.

(Adapted from *Sichos Mussar* #28, *Atzlus*, *Behar-Bechukosai*, 5732)

The Torah tells us that the princes of the Tribes, spiritually elevated individuals, brought the precious stones needed for the garments of the Kohein Gadol. Interestingly, the Torah mentions the contribution of these tribal leaders only after recounting the generosity of the Jewish laypeople. In addition, it leaves out a letter from their title: *nesi'im*, or princes, is spelled without the letter *yud*.

Citing a famous *midrash*, Rashi explains, "Rabi Nassan said: What did the princes see that made them contribute first to the inauguration of the Altar [occurring later, in *Bamidbar*], while they did not contribute first [here] in the construction of the *Mishkan*? The princes said, 'Let the public contribute whatever they contribute, and what is lacking from their contribution, we will supplement.' Since the public completed everything ... the princes said: 'What is there for us to do?' [So] 'They brought the precious stones...' Therefore, they [later] contributed first at the inauguration of the Altar. And because they were lazy at the outset, a letter [*yud*] was deleted from their name ..."

What was so lazy about the actions of the princes? Wasn't it noble and considerate of them to allow the masses to contribute first, pledging to complete whatever would be lacking at the end?

Some of the commentaries explain that the princes did, indeed, believe that their motivations were wholly pure. However, on a deeper, subconscious level, the true root of their inaction was laziness. This is what Rashi is telling us, and this is why they were censured by Hashem by losing a letter in their name. They had a ready rationalization, and it was even what they truly believed. But the Torah, which penetrates to the deepest levels of a person's heart to uncover the true motivations, reveals to us that even the princes, as spiritually great as they were, were swayed by laziness. They lagged in donating to the *Mishkan* because of their reluctance to take part in an energetic initiative.

We do see that the princes corrected that flaw, for at a later opportunity, they were the first to contribute. They repented their laziness and learned their lesson, and showed admirable *zerizus*, enthusiasm, and energy in their donations to the Altar.

Throughout the ages, our *gedolim* have always been wary of any hint of laziness in their decisions, and they always exerted themselves to excise the trait of laziness and destroy its hidden remnants.

> *There were times Rav Yosef Yoizel of Novardok needed to decide whether it was appropriate to attend a meeting in another city. On these occasions, Rav Yosef Yoizel made a point of actually going to the appropriate location before he made his decision. In this way, he could be sure that his choice was not motivated by laziness.*
>
> *For the same reason, when Rav Isser Zalmen Meltzer was asked to write a letter of recommendation on*

someone's behalf, he would first write the letter, then decided whether or not he actually wished to confer it.

(Bederch Eitz Chaim)

One evening, while Rav Yisroel Salanter was learning in the beis medrash, *he overheard a conversation between two poor people.*

"Would you please walk with me to the well so I can get a drink of water?" said one man to the other. "I am very thirsty but I'm afraid to walk alone in the dark."

"Not now," replied the second man, "I'm too tired to get up."

As soon as Rav Yisroel heard the man's request, he jumped from his seat, ran to the well and brought back a bottle of water.

(Tenuas Ha'mussar)

PRACTICAL ADVICE

- A person should complete a task before its assigned time. This applies to both material and spiritual concerns. Then, if some unexpected delay occurs, it is still possible to complete the duty on time.

- When doing such mundane tasks as eating, washing, and exercising, keep in mind that we are always committed to our mandate to serve Hashem. Use the time wisely and efficiently.

- One who studies in yeshivah should always be on time, for every moment is precious.

- Always walk to your destination swiftly.

- Too much sleep can be harmful, causing headaches. A person should determine how much sleep they need and sleep no more than required. (Rav Ben Zion Abba Shaul)

- Rav Shlomo Wolbe suggests that we try to fulfill at least three mitzvos a day with enthusiasm (*Alei Shur*, Vol. II).

- It is beneficial to write a schedule, starting with the time you wish to get up in the morning and continuing with all your activities.

- Leave early for all appointments.

- Fine yourself each time you fail in a commitment.

- Daven to Hashem for help.

* * *

The Alter of Kelm allowed himself only ten minutes to rise and get dressed.

When Rav Yehudah Tzadkah walked to the beit knesset with his children, he always maintained a quick pace and expected them to keep up with him. He explained that it is a mitzvah to run to do the service of Hashem, as it is written, "Let us run to know Hashem" (Hoshea 6:3). Even in his old age, when he no longer had much strength, Rav Yehudah made a point of hurrying for the last few steps before he entered the shul, saying to his grandchild who accompanied him, "Let us run to the house of Hashem!"

(Ve'zos Le'Yehudah)

Food For Thought

Rav Yechezkel of Kuzmir had a hard time keeping up with Rav Yitzchok of Vorke when they walked together. He asked his friend why he walked so quickly.

Rav Yitzchok replied, "A Jew must constantly be running, never simply walking. Either he is running to perform a mitzvah or running from a sin."

(Rosh Golas Ariel)

A Constant Struggle

Laziness is a devastating trait that can deprive us of both worlds. Everyone struggles with indolence, but it must be overcome, at any time and at any age. Initially, the damage it wreaks may not be readily apparent, but laziness slowly and insidiously mires a person in wickedness.

Rav Nosson Wachtfogel once arrived uncharacteristically late to davening in Beth Medrash Gavoha. In his humility, the Mashgiach *turned to a student and commented, "I was really lazy today."*

Surprised, the student exclaimed, "After so many years of enthusiastic fulfillment of mitzvos, the Mashgiach *is still dealing with the temptation of laziness?"*

The Mashgiach *retorted, "What do you mean? When a person gets older, he* shteigs *[advances] in laziness!"*

(Yated Neeman, 8 Kislev 5769)

The Tchebiner Rav asked his daughter to mail some money to a certain poor relative. She asked if it could wait, as she had some things to take care of at home before leaving. Her father replied that if she didn't go right now, he would go himself. He added, "A Jew must always be ready to set out at every given moment."

(Marbitzei Torah Me'olam Ha'chassidus)

The road to righteousness can be completely blocked by melancholy, which is laziness's cohort. This is the emotion that leads us to conclude that we cannot succeed or that a task is beyond our abilities. We must examine our actions to determine if they stem from melancholy, for dejection can penetrate different areas. When we become conscious of its sinister hand, we must fight it at all costs. (Rav Chaim Shmulevitz on *Atzlus*)

The Chofetz Chaim was quoted as saying, "One must always forge onward, make his best effort, and never lose hope. Even if he sees negligible results in his Torah study, or finds it difficult, to perform a mitzvah, he should still not give up, but continue his efforts. Success will come in it's own time — perhaps from a very unexpected source."

INSPIRATION

The *yetzer hara* tries five ways to prevent us from enthusiastically carrying out our deeds. He tells us:

- You have plenty of time
- The distance is limited
- The journey is uncomplicated

- The reward is insignificant
- The Master won't mind if the job remains undone

Rabi Tarfon dismisses all these five diversionary tactics when he says, "The day is short, the task is large, the laborers are lazy, the wage is great, and the Master of the house is insistent."

(*Yavetz* on *Avos* 3:20)

The Chasam Sofer points out that a task appears challenging when the laborers are lazy. However, when a person is enthusiastic about a project, the task appears uncomplicated.

The *Mesilas Yesharim* says that another manifestation of laziness, unwarranted fear, can sometimes prevent a person from undertaking a project. To justify his inaction, he blames external factors that are beyond his control, asserting that he is afraid that he might fail.

People tend to procrastinate because they link taking action with pain rather than comfort or pleasure. We must try to associate pleasure with accomplishment, and pain with neglect of responsibility. Relish the joy of doing something you find difficult. Ponder the unlimited possibilities of the rewards associated with keeping mitzvos. This will enable us to naturally commit ourselves to a task without wasting time.

The family of the Imrei Emes would serve his entire meal at once, including the cup of coffee he drank when he finished eating. His weekday meals never took more than seven minutes from start to finish. On Shabbos, the meal lasted 22 minutes. If the entire meal was not ready, he did not wait; he would eat what there was, bentch, *and return to his* seforim.

One day, the Rebbetzin apologized for the delay of part of the meal. "It was only one minute late," she excused herself.

The Rebbe asked with surprise, "Is one minute a small matter?"

(*Rosh Golas Ariel*, Part I, page 267)

The Gerrer Rebbe once attended a series of important meetings in the city of Lodz. In the two-hour break between two meetings, he ate lunch, participated in a Sefer Torah's *completion and accompanying festive meal, distributed "sharayim" to his chassidim, gave a short Torah lecture, visited two sick chassidim, participated in a* sheva berachos, *and attended a fundraiser for acquiring properties in Eretz Yisroel. He returned to the conference room precisely two minutes before the proceedings were scheduled to resume, and he was the first to arrive.*

(*Rosh Golas Ariel*, Part I, page 269)

Rav Chaim Shmulevitz would take his meals while learning with a partner. While he ate, his learning partner would speak. The meal lasted no more than three to five minutes. His Shabbos meals lasted a bit longer.

One year, when the yeshivah was in Japan, one of the locals invited himself for the afternoon

Shabbos seudah. *After davening, the man got involved in a conversation that lasted fifteen minutes.*

Rav Chaim walked into the beis medrash. *The man, thinking that Rav Chaim had come to call him, hurried to apologize for the delay.* "I am coming," *he promised.*

"There is no need for you to hurry," *Rav Chaim calmly replied.* "Your meal is waiting for you, but I have already eaten. You can join me for the third Shabbos meal instead."

(*Moach Ve'lev*, Chapter 8)

INSPIRATION

Procrastination is the characteristic of Amalek. "Moshe said to Yehoshua, 'Select for us people and go fight Amalek. *Tomorrow* I will stand on the top of the hill'" (*Shemos* 17:9). It is unclear whether the word "tomorrow" refers to the fighting or the standing (*Yoma* 22). Either way, the word is superfluous. It appears in the verse because it represents the intrigues of the *yetzer hara*. He encourages us to delay the performance of mitzvos until tomorrow. Then, he changes tomorrow to after tomorrow. The more time passes, the less likely it becomes that one will actually do the mitzvah.

(Rav Yosef Chaim Sonnenfeld)

If you do not feel any enthusiasm for the service of Hashem, Rav Michel of Lechovitz suggests that you force yourself to serve Hashem anyway, even in an artificially enthusiastic manner. The soul within you flickers like a flame and you can generate fuel for the flame even with false excitement. Meditate on the possibilities inherent in each mitzvah. Recall deeds that excited you. Then think, speak, and act as you would if you were truly enthusiastic.

Every morning, the *yetzer hara* struggles to keep us in bed so there is less time for Torah and prayer. From the moment you awaken, think thoughts of self-discipline instead of laziness. Rav Yisroel Salanter noted that in these private moments, you can serve Hashem in the ultimate manner simply by rising from your bed with alacrity.

> *Even on the day of his death, Rav Simcha Zissel Ziv mustered his strength and jumped out of bed for fear that perhaps his weakness stemmed from laziness. He aroused his small children early in the morning gently with the words, "Kinderlach, you're sleeping away a kingdom!" for Hashem appointed man king over Creation.*
>
> (*Sparks of Mussar*, page 74)

Don't get irritated over trivialities. Know your priorities so you use your limited time, energy, and resources in the most efficient manner. (Piaseczne Rebbe; Rabbi Zelig Pliskin, *Begin Again Now, Consulting the Wise*)

> *Rav Salmon Mutzafi insisted that any bris he attended, whether as* mohel *or* sandak, *should take place as early as possible. "Zerizin makdimin l'mitzvos," he said. "We must perform mitzvos with alacrity." He maintained that our generation's pathetic performance in the areas of Torah and fear of Hashem could be*

attributed to the fact that the very first mitzvah to which baby boys are exposed is all too often delayed.

(Olamo Shel Tzaddik)

The Steipler's time was so valuable that when he was served soup that was too hot to consume, he simply poured cold water into the bowl so he could eat it as quickly as possible. If he had to wait at a family simchah, he sat in a corner and learned. Another mishnah, another perek — whatever he could.

Late one Shabbos afternoon, a young man entered his room and found the Steipler standing near a window, trying to catch enough light learn another few lines in Pri Megadim before it got dark.

(Hochmas Koherel, Part II, page 63)

Rav Shmuel Markowitz passed Rav Shach and found him deep in thought. When Rav Shach noticed him, he said, "Do you know what I am thinking about now? I am thinking about what needs to be done tomorrow and considering if it is possible to do any of those things today."

(Kinyan Torah)

A young man once asked Rav Chaim Kanievsky how he manages to receive so many people in an hour.

Rav Chaim replied, "There are 60 minutes in an hour and 60 seconds in a minute. That is 3,600 *seconds. Do you know how much can be done in 3,600 seconds?"*

(Tuvcha Yabiu, Part II, page 134)

Food For Thought

Laziness stems from sadness. Connect with Hashem and you will achieve happiness and, eventually, *zerizus*. (Baal Ha'Tanya) When a person fulfills a mitzvah with *zerizus*, he announces to the world how important the mitzvah is to him. (*Seforno, Vayeirah* 18:2)

Balancing Deliberation And Alacrity

Are you being deliberate or lazy? As with most character traits, you must aspire to the correct balance. A righteous person is compared to the sun; just as the sun whitens clothing that has been hung to dry and darkens the skin at the same time, a virtuous individual avails himself of enthusiasm or sluggishness, depending on the situation. (*Od Yosef Chai*)

Food For Thought

Most sins result from acting too hastily. If a person were to reflect on what he is about to do, he would not sin. Unfortunately, his *yetzer hara* urges him to act swiftly, so he has no time to contemplate what he is doing. Only afterward, when it is too late, does he regret the deed.

(Ateres Le'rosh Tzaddik)

A person with a quick nature must be careful to avoid acting swiftly without reflection. This is referred to as *pezizus*. A person who moves unthinkingly is usually not orderly, often buys the first thing he sees, does not stop to think, and will study lots of material in superficial manner. He often says the first thing that occurs to him without stopping to consider if it will hurt someone

Food For Thought

We are taught that the *Shechinah* cannot rest where there is laziness (*Shabbos* 31). We are also taught that a person who embraces laziness when subject to temptation, and thereby does not sin, is sustained by the *Shechinah*'s radiance.

(*Kallah* 1:17)

How can we know if an act stems from *zerizus* or from *pezizus*? How do we know if our alacrity is inspired by our good inclination or driven by the desires of our evil inclination?

EXERCISE

- Use a notebook to record verses, *midrashim*, and other relevant sayings and review them regularly.

- Do you tend to react hastily? Before you speak, ask yourself if there is any value in what you are about to say.

- Place notes all over your house and in your wallet as reminders: "Don't be lazy!"

- If you are learning, don't pause to look up when someone enters the room.

- Never buy impulsively.

- Try to complete everything you begin. Finish learning the amount you have set for yourself, and when you are finished, ask yourself if you studied it superficially or with proper depth.

- When you catch yourself davening speedily, slow down.

⚬ ⚬

Rav Aharon Kotler was constantly on guard against laziness. He was always fearful that he wasn't doing enough.

It once happened that after a particularly grueling day, Rav Aharon told his Rebbetzin that he wanted to rest for a short time. A few moments later, the Rebbetzin peeked into the bedroom. She was surprised to see that the Rosh Yeshivah was sitting on the bed, and she asked him why he wasn't lying down.

The Rosh Yeshivah answered, "Ich klehr efsher iz dos atzlus – I'm thinking about it. Maybe it's just laziness!"

(*The Legacy of Maran Rav Aharon Kotler*, page 489)

Food For Thought

There are two aspects to the *yetzer hara*: fire and water. He either inflames us with overpowering desire to do an *aveirah*, or cools our enthusiasm for mitzvos with laziness. We must counter the *yetzer hara* by using the water aspect of Torah to cool our passions, and the fire aspect of Torah to inspire mitzvah performance.

(Magid of Mezritch, cited by
Mayan Ha'nitzchi, Ki Seitze)

When the Sanzer Rav davened, his thundering voice exuded such fiery enthusiasm that all who heard his devotions would feel their hearts melt.

On the other hand, when involved in mundane matters, his acts were performed perfunctorily, without any emphasis on his routine.

The Noda Be'Yehudah was once asked if hunting was permissible. The questioner wondered if it be might forbidden to inflict pain on animals he did not intend to consume. The Noda Be'Yehudah responded at length to the halachic query, but at the bottom of the response, he added a footnote: "I can't help but ask. How do you have time to hunt?"

INSPIRATION

"For the sin that we have sinned before You with legs that run to do evil" (*Vidui* prayer). Why refer to the legs as running on their own? When a person greatly desires something, it is almost as if his feet start moving reflexively before he even has time to think.

Conversely, a truly righteous person such as David Ha'melech will find his feet taking him to the *beis medrash*, even when he had originally planned to go elsewhere.

(Vayikra Rabbah)

Generally, desire is stronger than intellect. Love and hate are known to interfere with people's thought processes. Desire has a way of forcing us to take action. *Ratzon,* the word for desire, includes the word *ratz,* which means run. Lavan loved money, and therefore rushed to greet Yaakov.

There are times when we must take a quantum leap to attach ourselves to the desired spiritual goal, acting quickly to preserve that momentum. Then we can resume a deliberate mindset. A person who acts on his thoughts immediately is one who understands the power of the *yetzer hara* to interfere with the performance of good deeds.

There is a well-known story about a yeshivah student who was asked a question in the middle of a meal. Distressed at being unable to answer the question, he ran to the *beis medrash* and threw himself into intense study for seven years. Rav Chaim Shmuelevitz questions whether or not he did the right thing. He points out that although he should have *bentched* first, there is no doubt that he would have missed the singular opportunity to grow had he put off his resolution for even a moment.

Food For Thought

Those who act quickly will often fail. For the most part, people who work very quickly do a second-rate, superficial job without the proper attentiveness. Rav Avrohom Grodzinsky defined *zerizus* as carefully plotting out your moves. We must always remember to keep the proper balance, putting all our effort into what we are doing and working as conscientiously and efficiently as possible. (Piaseczne Rebbe) This results in improving your success rate.

INSPIRATION

David Ha'melech personified the characteristic of alacrity.

David was disturbed by knowing that he lived in a house of cedar wood, while the holy *Aron* was housed in a structure of curtains. He summoned Nassan Ha'navi and poured out his heart to him, requesting permission to begin construction of the *Beis Ha'mikdash*. (*II Shmuel* 7:2)

Nassan gave him immediate approval: "Whatever is in your heart, go and do, for Hashem is with you." (ibid, 7:3)

However, that very night Nassan received a prophecy from Hashem, ordering him to return to the palace and tell David that he would not be allowed to build the *Beis Ha'mikdash*. It would be built by his son Shlomo instead.

Rashi explains that Nassan was ordered to return to the palace immediately because Hashem knew of David's zeal in performing mitzvos. "The man [David] is quick and will be hiring workers and ordering building supplies. If you don't stop him now, you will cause him great loss when he has to cancel the project after so many arrangements have been made."

Deliberation can sometimes originate from a negative source. The Chazon Ish taught that one who flaunts his moderation and despises commitment is either a hypocrite or unintelligent. Rav Yosef Leib Bloch was annoyed at those who preached moderation and deliberation in spiritual matters. He felt that their call for prudence stemmed from their lack of devotion to Hashem, not to a true sense of caution. If someone were to threaten their honor or their pocketbooks, they would no longer advocate calm rather than action!

A businessman often tarried in shul after prayers. One day, a purchaser arrived at his home. His wife informed the potential customer that her husband had not yet returned. Unable to wait, the man made his purchases elsewhere.

When he heard that he had lost out on a lucrative deal, the businessman was very annoyed. He instructed his wife that in the future, she was to come to the shul to call him when customers came to their home.

A few days later, when a man knocked on the door looking for her husband, she ran to get him. Her husband rushed home together with her, only to discover that the waiting man was a creditor.

Angrily turning on his wife, he exclaimed, "What is wrong with you? When a creditor calls you rush to bring me home, but when a customer comes knocking you can't be bothered to call me?"

(Shaar Bas Rabim)

Food For Thought

The Imrei Emes looked on his watch as a most trusted companion. He once he gave his watch to the watchmaker to be repaired because it fell behind a few seconds each day. When a young newlywed came to the Rebbe to ask which *mussar* text he should study, the Imrei Emes pointed to his watch and said, "This is the biggest *mussar* text — every minute that passes never comes back."

The Imrei Emes often remarked, "Why do we give a bridegroom a gold watch as a gift? To teach him that each minute and second is worth more than gold."

(Rosh Golas Ariel, page 263)

Personal Growth

Planning Ahead

No one is born with perfect character traits. Even the most refined individuals must fine-tune their character traits to achieve the proper balance. A person born with a warm heart has to work on being strict when necessary, and rebuking when appropriate. A person who is naturally hasty has to force himself to give thoughtful consideration to whether a deed should be pursued or avoided. A person who is naturally charitable has to learn not to fritter away his money on others. A person who is naturally humble must be careful to safeguard the honor of another to the extreme.

It is true that some of our character traits require only nominal upgrading, but even individuals whose characters require a lot of polishing are capable of exhibiting superior character traits on given occasions, or when interacting with specific individuals. Everyone is enthusiastic about projects they enjoy. Everyone has a good heart when it comes to doing favors for people they like. Some are vigilant when it comes to distributing charity; others are careful about beautifying a mitzvah. Every individual pursues his preference, careful about those things he considers important.

Do not attempt to go completely against your nature. Instead, labor to channel character traits down the path of your designing. Take those good traits that occasionally manifest themselves and build on them! Then find the character traits you need to correct and work on them. Do not allow the negative traits you find to bring you to despair. Bad traits can be corrected; good traits were given to us to perfect them. This is our job in this world.

Don't move aimlessly, from one target to another. Create an incremental, interconnected plan for working on yourself. Each undertaking should prepare you for the next phase in your personal growth.

Food For Thought

Many good character traits are intertwined. For example, humility is connected to calmness, compassion to generosity, contentment to abstinence, and so on.

(*Ha'maspik Le'ovdei Hashem*)

Since all character traits are interconnected, working on one will automatically have a positive effect on all others.

(Chazon Ish)

Each of us possess a measure of rebelliousness deep within. It's like a metal coil: when given the chance, it can spring into action and wreak havoc. Any program of personal growth must take this into consideration. Always stay ahead of your inner sense of rebelliousness. When you feel that you are being choked by a spiritual change you have undertaken, it's a sign that it's time to move on.

Move forward at a steady pace, but proceed cautiously at first, until you reach a point where you feel capable of an all-out effort to fully attain a spiritual goal. Confident that you can succeed? Then move ahead, bravely and enthusiastically.

The Piaseczne Rebbe, Rabbi Kalonymos Kalman Shapiro, compares character improvement to fighting a carefully planned war, where strategy is developed based on honest and thorough research. See what is really holding back improvement, and then overcome the barrier. If one tactic does not work, try another and yet another. Persistence and hard work — never deserting the battlefield — will, with Hashem's help, certainly bring success.

No Embarrasment

The only way to achieve greatness is to turn a blind eye to the opinions of others. You will not be able to work on yourself if you are always conscious of what everyone else thinks. Serve Hashem with courage and self-assurance!

While learning in Lithuania, Rav Nosson Mayer Wachtfogel made the effort to visit the Chofetz Chaim. In an hour-long lecture on the topic of serving Hashem independently, the Chofetz Chaim spoke about not imitating others and never looking over our shoulders at what others are doing. He spoke against "going with the flow" and taking other people's opinions too seriously.

Rochel, the wife of Rabi Akiva, taught this concept to her husband. When she first suggested that he go learn Torah, he replied, "People will laugh at me — I am forty years old and I know nothing!" He was concerned that he would have to join the children studying alef-beis with their teacher, and he would become the butt of their laughter.

Rochel understood her husband's concerns, and came up with an idea that would enable him to overcome his embarrassment. She sent him to buy a donkey that had been so overworked it had developed deep holes between the vertebrae of its spine. The donkey was readily acquired for a pittance, for it was not serviceable any more.

Rochel filled the spaces with earth and planted some quick growing herbs. In a short time, these herbs were proliferating in the dirt — in fact, they appeared to be growing right out of the donkey's back! Rochel then asked Rabi Akiva to take the donkey outside.

The first time, everyone gathered around, pointing and laughing at the strange sight. The second time there was more of the same. But by the third day, people had gotten used to the sight of a flowering donkey, and no one was laughing anymore. They had grown accustomed to this new variety of donkey.

Rochel had made her point. Even the most unusual sight will arouse amusement only for a brief period of time before people get used to it. Rabi Akiva was convinced that he could succeed.

(Midrash Ha'gadol, Shemos 4:13)

The Alter of Novardok ingrained his students with such strength of character that they were neither embarrassed nor afraid of anyone. They were firm as a rock before all mockery, refusing to concede their viewpoint to anyone. One could find Novardokers standing on a platform in the marketplace, exhorting their audience to leave their temporary lives and devote themselves to eternal life. They could be seen ascending at a meeting of communists, to lecture enthusiastically on the worthlessness of a life of vanity and to advocate a return to spirituality. And a group of students joined in public debate with the Yevesktzia (members of the Jewish department of the communist party) on the Jewish religion, strongly refuting all the arguments of the opposition.

(*Giants of Jewry II*, pages 125–126)

Small Steps

Ready to strive for closeness to Hashem? The key is to begin your program of personal growth immediately. It's natural to resist getting started, because it means that we must be prepared for drastic changes in our lives.

Food For Thought

Mussar shreit, gevald, beit zich! The study of *mussar* shouts, "Change!"

(Rav Chaim Shmulevitz)

How to begin? The task of character development seems overwhelming. We observe where we are, think about where we want to be, note the gap between the two — and we realize the difficulty of the task. This is why we are advised to progress slowly, step by step.

Don't give up because the task is too hard. Break the challenge into small pieces. Focus on small changes, day by day; turn the task into manageable units. This will prevent collapsing under unnaturally high standards caused by moving too quickly to levels you're not ready for. (Rabbi Abraham Twerski)

INSPIRATION

"Wisdom is before the understanding one, and the eyes of the fool are at the edge of the earth" (*Mishlei* 17:24). Rashi explains that the fool insists that wisdom is not accessible; it is far away from him. "How can I learn all of *Nezikin*, which is thirty chapters, and *Keilim*, also thirty, and *Shabbos*, which is twenty-four?"

But for the wise man it is easy. Today he learns two chapters, tomorrow another two. He says, "This is the way of those who lived before me in the world."

Taking on too much at once — trying to change ourselves too quickly — is counterproductive. Yaakov saw a "ladder planted in the ground whose top reached the heavens, and behold there were angels of G-d going up and going down it." If we try to ascend and swiftly transform ourselves into angels — become *"malachei Elokim olim"* — we risk falling right back down — *"ve'yordim bo."*

(*Bereishis* 28:12; Klausenberger Rebbe)

It is important not to undertake too many commitments at once. Rav Wolbe gives some practical advice on how to develop character, little by little:

- Learning kindness. Do three small acts of kindness each day. After a couple of months you will start developing sensitivity to people — seeing what they need, thinking of how to help them.

- *Kavanah* in prayer. Begin by concentrating on every word of the first two blessings of the Shemoneh Esrei for several months. Then add more, until you eventually reach a whole davening with *kavanah*.

- Anger. Instead of just resolving to be patient and never lose your temper, try taking on a half hour of patience every day. Rav Wolbe suggests doing this at a critical time, such as right before coming home in the evening. Try it for a couple of months, moving around this half hour throughout the day, so you have practice being patient in many different situations.

- Concentration. This is a particularly difficult area, so starting small is crucial. Try going to a quiet place. For just five minutes, focus on one thing without letting any foreign thoughts distract you. After a couple of weeks move to eight minutes, then ten. Finally, try focusing your thoughts while walking in the street or in a situation where there are distractions.

Getting To Know Ourselves

We all possess every possible character trait to one degree or another. Some traits are barely noticeable; others are so strong that they essentially define us. We each possess one positive trait that is the foundation of our personality and behavior, and a specific negative trait that can detrimentally affect every one of our *middos*. The strong *middah* should ideally be used to protect our good deeds and traits, while controlling the weaker part of our personality.

Discovering these basic, root *middos* is the first step towards self-knowledge, for they are the foundations of our personality and behavior.

INSPIRATION

Only through guiding our naturally good attributes can man achieve perfection. In truth, the entire foundation of man's service is through the good attributes he naturally possesses. If he guards them and grasps them properly, never losing his natural goodness, he will attain his goal of perfecting his intelligence. Even his negative nature and *middos* will turn to become completely good.

Reuven buys a vessel from a non Jew and then sells it to Shimon, believing it to be an inexpensive metal container. Shimon later discovers that it is pure silver. Does Shimon have to pay Reuven more money?

Shimon owes Reuven nothing. Since Reuven was unaware that he had a silver vessel, he never really owned a silver vessel. The same applies to a person who is unaware of his true greatness; he therefore has no greatness.

(Hagahos Ashri, Bava Metzia 2)

Identifying these two traits puts us on the road to perfection, because we now know what Hashem wants us to work on. How do we identify them? Note which *middah* exists in all your actions, under all circumstances. If you can find that *middah*, you will know that you have found your core character trait.

For example, a child always tells the truth, even if this will bring him punishment. This child is gifted with the trait of truthfulness. A person who finds great joy in helping others — even when it is difficult for him — possesses the *middah* of kindness. One who pays careful attention to detail in all his commitments, has the *middah* of strength.

PRACTICAL ADVICE

Asking yourself certain questions helps you determine your strengths.

- I feel best when ...
- My highest aspiration is to ...
- The idea that has helped me the most is ...
- I respect people who ...

(*Begin Again Now*, pages 312–313, Rabbi Zelig Pliskin)

EXERCISE

Make a list of the traits you feel you have. Put on the top of the list the trait you believe you excel in. Place at the bottom the trait that you feel is your weakest.

Rabbi Chaim Vital writes that there are four foundations to all character traits, corresponding to the four fundamental elements of fire, water, air, and dust (earth).

Fire represents one's intellect and corresponds to the desire to ascend in life and rule. Negative examples are haughtiness, anger, rigid authority, demanding honor, hatred, and stubbornness. Positive examples are modesty, humility, flexibility, and restraint.

Air represents the power of speech. In the negative, it manifests itself as idle chatter, flattery, lies, slander, and gossip. In its positive manifestation, it is seen in one who says only what is necessary, is quick to praise, speaks about Torah thoughts, and provides emotional support for others.

Water represents the spiritual background of the vital soul. A person forged from this character foundation will show a preference for physical pleasures — lusting after money and with a love of self-indulgence. He also is likely to be jealous. When he has channeled this tendency to the good, he will feel disgust in the face of unneeded physical pleasures and will be a trusting, caring individual.

Dust corresponds to the spirituality of the body and will manifest itself as sadness, grief, laziness, and hopelessness in its negative manifestations. Individuals possessed of its positive expression are satisfied with what they have, and serve Hashem with happiness.

Some character traits consist of more than one fundamental. An example of this is mocking others, which results from air (slander/cruelty) and fire (haughtiness). (*Rabbeinu Yonah*)

Identifying The Source

We need to identify the *middos* that drive our actions. There are some obvious imperfections. We get angry and petulant. We are egocentric and stingy. We love to dominate. We view others as means to our own ends. We are selfish and envious of others. We speak ill of other people. We chase after things that do us no good. We are lazy and often childish and impatient. We believe in our hearts that we deserve much more than what we have. We idolize power and money.

But while these traits may be obvious to others, a person finds it very hard to see anything wrong in himself.

> *While still a young man, Rav Chaim Shmuelevitz was asked to address a group of scholars at a beis ha'mussar. As he rose to speak, he detected an undercurrent of doubt as to his capacity to deliver a lecture to their satisfaction.*
>
> *He began, "I am the most outstanding scholar in this generation."*
>
> *They looked at him in stunned disbelief.*
>
> *"I am the most outstanding scholar in this generation," he repeated, his voice growing louder, "and anyone who doesn't listen to me has a status of a rebellious authority!"*
>
> *By now his voice was a roar. The audience stared at him with a mixture of curiosity and scorn.*
>
> *"That is what every single person in this room believes about himself!"*
>
> *All at once, there was no more cynicism — only a*

humble willingness to listen to this man who seemed to understand them.

(From an article on Rav Chaim Shmuelevitz by Yisroel Besser, *Mishpacha*, Issue 239)

Food For Thought

A person who has not labored to identify and correct his negative character traits is like a blind person who has never seen light.

(Rav Yisroel Salanter)

Beginnings are the root of everything. So try looking back as far as you can. What are you afraid of? What is easy for you? What do you avoid doing? These questions enable us to know ourselves. You will come to understand how your past experiences affect the way you are today, and to better know your inner self.

One who knows himself will know what he needs to fix in life. Try breaking down your actions into separate parts to determine which character traits are present in that action. What makes you angry? What calms you down? What makes you jealous of certain people? Why are you not jealous of other people?

When the spies came back with a detailed description of unusually large vegetation (*Bamidbar* 13), Rashi adds significant details. "Just as their fruits are extraordinary, so is the nation [that dwells there]." In other words, there is no way of conquering these people.

The *Zohar* explains that in the inner recesses of their hearts, the *meraglim* thought, "If the Jewish People enter Eretz Yisroel, they will no longer require our services and Moshe Rabbeinu will appoint others in our place" (*Shelach* 158).

How tragic! Their desire to maintain their prestige resulted in the death of the entire generation.

This was not a conscious calculation. If you had confronted them, they would have stuck to their arguments that capturing the land is easier said than done. But our Sages looked into their hearts and identified their true motives. (*Mesilas Yesharim* 11)

Another example lies within the episode of Korach. Korach claimed that all Jews are holy and required no elite priestly caste to rule them. He even went so far as to encourage the firstborns to retake the privilege of serving in the *Beis Ha'mikdash*. (*Bamidbar* 16:3; see Rashi and Ibn Ezra ad loc.)

Rashi explains that Korach acted out of jealousy (*Bamidbar* 16:1). What touched off his rebellion was the appointment of Elizaphan as head of the tribe of Levi. If Amram's sons were appointed king and Kohein, surely it was only right that he, as the son of Amram's next younger brother, should receive the honor of being selected as head of the tribe.

While this was his thought process, his action was ostensibly motivated by his desire to address an injustice against the Jewish nation. The whole rebellion started because of an inner feeling of jealousy that went out of control.

We must constantly be on the lookout for how our *middos* affect our thoughts, speech, and action. Because the power of our *middos* is buried deep inside, it may be impossible to fully reveal them — even through hard work.

Before beginning a program of personal growth, most of us remain unaware of the many thoughts that enter our minds and the subconscious, despite the fact that these feelings and thoughts affect our actions and the way we interact with our surroundings.

> *One of Rav Chaim Shmuelevitz's students brought a younger brother who was seeking acceptance to the yeshivah to meet Rav Chaim.*
>
> *Rav Chaim turned to the older brother, a close student of his, and asked if the younger brother knew how to learn. The older brother, uncomfortable with the question, shrugged. "I haven't been in yeshivah with him for several years. I really don't know."*
>
> *Rav Chaim was astonished. "How can a person say that he doesn't know his own brother?"*
>
> *Then, wishing to take the edge off his criticism, he reflected aloud, "But then again, does a person know his own self?"*

This is why we must ask ourselves, "What is really causing me to do this?" Listen to the way you justify your actions. For example, what prevents a person from davening with devotion? It may be lack of inner peace, lack of patience, deficient faith; it might be conceit, selfishness, or simply lack of discipline. Trace your action to its source, so you can begin to address the actual cause.

Improper diagnosis leads to unproductive character improvement. How to improve a situation depends on what the real source of the problem is.

Rav Kalonymus Kalman Shapira, the Piaseczne Rebbe, offers two examples.

A person is angry. There are a number of possible sources of his anger. He might be hotheaded. But, says Rav Kalonymous Kalman, his anger might actually stem from his arrogance.

Because he looks down on others, he thinks nothing of speaking harshly to them — just as someone might hit or scream at an animal to get it moving. If this person wants to change, taking advice on how to prevent hotheaded behavior will not help him conquer his problem. For his character flaw is rooted in arrogance; it is only manifesting itself in anger.

Two people are arrogant, but the sources of their arrogance are completely different. The first has a bloated image of himself, while the second simply has not had contact with people who are greater than he. The solution to the second person's problem is much simpler than that of the first. If he meets great tzaddikim or lamdanim, he will see himself in perspective; if he reads of the high standards that appear in sifrei mussar, or in the biographies of gedolei Torah, he will realize that he has much to learn. The same phenomenon, but very different sources and very different methods of change

Food For Thought

The exuberance that is the by-product of self-control animates the individual. It is the most pleasurable feeling to reign in our animalistic instincts. This effort energizes our souls, time and again, in a delightful manner.

(*Letters of the Chazon Ish*, part 2, letter 13)

Identifying our problems requires effort. What appears to be insolence can actually be courage. Shame may be sadness in disguise. A person who does not know his strengths and weaknesses cannot begin to work on self-improvement.

Your friend says, "Let me introduce you to the Rebbetzin, perhaps she will know of a shidduch for you." You reply, "Please don't. I'm too shy." Perhaps what you are defining as shyness is actually despair.

Pay attention to your words and the thoughts behind those words. Recognize how various thoughts take root. Listen to the way you explain your actions. When did you start feeling that way? How did your attitude change?

A journal is an invaluable tool to self knowledge. Record the events and thoughts that touched you, or anything of lasting value.

Food For Thought

The first gateway into the service of Hashem is that man knows his self-worth and recognizes his strengths and the strengths of his forefathers, their greatness and importance to the Creator. He must say, "I am a great and important man who possesses many good and exalted traits, the son of greatness and royalty. How can I possibly commit evil and sin to my G-d and my forefathers?"

If, heaven forbid, we do not recognize our greatness and the greatness of our forefathers, it will be easy to follow immoral paths and relentlessly seek to indulge our base urges.

(Rabbeinu Yonah, *Shaarei Ha'avodah*)

A selfish person should not focus on frugality. A lazy person should not focus on patience. If it is difficult for you to lend your possessions, focus on love for your fellow Jew. If you cannot keep a secret, then work on the trait of silence. Have difficulty telling the truth? Work on humility.

It is easy to make mistakes when it comes to using our character traits appropriately—when, how, and in what measure? The measure of a *middah* depends on the wisdom of each person. Which of your character traits is out of balance? Are you too lazy, too stingy, too disorganized, not self-disciplined enough? Determine which trait is out of sync, then go to the opposite extreme: be extremely diligent, giving, organized, disciplined. You will eventually become a balanced individual.

Balanced character traits are ideal. The only exceptions—traits that should be carried to an extreme—are avoiding arrogance and anger. (Rambam, *Mishneh Torah, Hilchos Deios*, Chapters 1–2)

When Eliezer, the servant of Avrohom, went on his mission to search for a bride for Yitzchok, the Alter of Novardok notes that Eliezer had to fight his inner desire: he actually wanted Yitzchok to marry his own daughter. This is derived from the way the word "perhaps" is written in the verse, "Perhaps the woman shall not wish to follow me to this land" (Bereishis 24:5). Written without the letter "vav," the word reads "to me" and expresses Eliezer's desire that Yitzchok marry his daughter.

Because he was aware that his own personal agenda might color his decisions on this important mission, Eliezer recognized the value of moving to the opposite extreme.

- He prayed for help, instead of relying on Avrohom's prayers on his behalf.
- He gave Rivkah the jewelry even before he knew who she was.
- He insisted on leaving immediately with Rivkah, not allowing any time for her to put together a trousseau.

Eliezer moved as swiftly as possible to fulfill Avrohom's request and successfully complete his mission.

(*Madreigas Ha'adam*; *Yalku Lekach Tov*, Vol. 1, *Chayei Sorah, Tikun Ha'middos Keizad*)

Tweaking Negative Tendencies

It is sometimes possible to channel negative tendencies into positive actions. Knowing of Eisav's bloodthirsty tendencies, Yitzchok sent him to hunt for food so he could direct his blood lust to appropriate ends. (Vilna Gaon)

Another possibility is to use one negative character trait to overcome another. Someone may be unwilling to give *tzedakah*, but the honor he receives as a result induces him to part with his money. In this case, the desire for honor overpowers the desire to hold on to one's money.

> *The Alter of Slobodka would tell the story of a peddler selling beans in the market. She got into an argument with a lady in a nearby stand and began cursing her loudly. It seemed that nothing could calm down.*
>
> *Suddenly a customer approached her stand, requesting a penny's worth of beans. It was astonishing to see how her entire demeanor changed: her face lit up, a smile turned up her lips, and she courteously turned to the lady and served her. Rav Nosson Tzvi learned from this incident that the craving for money can instantly prevail over the emotion of anger.*

Sometimes it is possible to sidestep the negative tendency and tackle it in an indirect fashion. Someone who is quick to anger should look for opportunities to do acts of *chesed*. Because he is focused on altruistic goals, he is less likely to succumb to his feelings of rage.

PRACTICAL SUGGESTIONS FOR CHANGE

Keeping Track

Keep a small notebook handy throughout the day. Make a list of positive character traits. Each time you practice it successfully, put a check next to that item; if you fail to make the grade, put a dot next to that attribute. By noting our successes and failures we acquire an awareness of what is happening and can more readily make the necessary changes.

Reviewing your chart will make it possible for you to identify weaknesses and work on self-improvement. This finger on your spiritual pulse enables you to note when your spiritual pressure is going down. And keeping a written record of your failures will enable you to stand up to the *yetzer hara*, who tries to persuade you that you are doing just fine. This written chart will also concretize your understanding of the fact that all our deeds are recorded. (*Avos* 2:1)

Forty Day Focus

Once you have chosen a character trait you wish to work on, take forty days and focus on that particular character problem (Rebbe Elimelech of Lizhensk in the *Tzetel Katan*).

Mussar and Introspection

Set aside time for introspection and the study of *mussar*. The requirement of daily ethical learning appears in the *Mishnah Berurah* (603:2), who traces it back to the Arizal. Commenting on the Rosh's suggestion to review Rabbeinu Yonah's Letter on *teshuvah* during the Ten Days of Repentance, he writes: "The Arizal writes that there is an obligation to learn ethical works all year (not only during the ten days between Rosh Ha'shanah and Yom Kippur), and the Gra mentions this in his commentary on *Mishlei* in a number of places."

The impact of daily learning and introspection may not be immediately apparent, but it will become evident over the course of time.

The Chasam Sofer would begin his daily shiurim *with the study of* mussar *and* middos *from the* sefer *Chofos Ha'levavos or the like. As a result, he merited students who were exceptional in all areas.*

(Rav Naftali Banet *in his eulogy of the Chasam Sofer*)

Copy and clip passages that you find helpful. I have a friend who keeps changing the clippings on her refrigerator.

Learning Relevant Halachos

Learn the halachos directly related to the character issues you are working on, to imprint its requirements on your psyche (*Igeres Ha'mussar*).

Internal Impact with Excitement

To impact our inner selves, the *gedolei mussar* taught, a sense of excitement is necessary. Rav Yisroel Salanter would say that "learning *mussar* with great excitement will merit one to learn his inner truths."

Food For Thought

Rav Yisroel Salanter wrote that *mussar* "transforms one into another person."

(*Letters, Ohr Yisroel* 10)

> "The sole thing that put me on my feet in matters
> of Hashem's service is *mussar* study ... Any day that I
> learn *mussar*, all my actions, speech, and thoughts are
> better."
>
> (Rav Naftali Amsterdam)

Rav Naftali Amsterdam divides the study of *mussar* into two stages: the comprehension stage, and the internalization stage.

The initial stage of understanding and comprehension uses the same intellectual processes that other Torah learning requires. Learn passages from *Mesilas Yesharim, Chovos Ha'levavos*, and similar *mussar* works via analysis, connecting to broader themes, and problem solving.

The second stage, internalization and inspiration, works differently. Take a short passage of *Pirkei Avos, Mesilas Yesharim*, or *Reishis Chochmah*, and learn it excitedly, repeating the words over and over again. Repeating the passages that particularly move you will bring about internalization of the concepts you are seeking to master.

Keep in mind that the *yetzer hara* is more likely to lead us astray by using externally acquired aspects of our personality. That which has been assimilated internally is not subject to being misled.

For example, if the desire to daven with a minyan is external to an individual, the *yetzer hara* will be able to persuade him that while going to minyan is admirable, today he must nurse his cold and stay home. But if he has internalized this need, he will not be easily persuaded to stay home.

Recognize that if your inner desire conflicts with the positive action, you will end up assisting the *yetzer hara* in coming up with excuses to alleviate your pangs of conscience. The *yetzer hara* will join us in our search for bad character traits and steer us away from the areas that really need searching. Investigate your deeds to ensure that you are not unconsciously seeking ways to avoid service of Hashem. (*Michtav Me'Eliyahu*)

> *It is like the story of the government agent who went to check a house that was suspected of containing an illegal distillery. With a smile the owner of the house greeted the agent and showed him through the house. The owner was extremely helpful, bending to look here and stretching to look there. Impressed by the man's helpfulness, the agent followed him faithfully. When they reached the place where the illegal operations were being carried out, the owner gently steered the agent aside in a friendly manner, saying, "Here there is nothing to look for."*
>
> *In such a search not only will the* middos *remain tainted, but the person will even fool himself into thinking that he has repented!"*
>
> (Alter of Novardok, *Sparks of Mussar*, page 140)

Outward Changes

Our hearts go after our actions; our inner lives are influenced by our outer lives. Changing the action will bring about a change in our character. (*Sefer Ha'chinuch*, in explaining many of the Torah's practical mitzvos)

For example, to improve the quality of your *berachos*, try washing your hands and sitting down before saying the *berachah*. Repeating these actions will make them second nature. (Rambam, *Hilchos Deios* 1:11)

> *When a student at the Kelmer Talmud Torah jumped over a gate to unlock a door, the Alter asked him to leave the yeshivah. He explained that a person who actively breaches fences will ultimately breach the safeguards set up by our Sages.*

Setting Up Barriers

Create an artificial barrier to certain sins for a specific length of time. Self-imposed fines is a good option. (*Chovas Ha'adam Be'olamo*)

This advice is often given to individuals attempting to give up smoking. They fine themselves for each cigarette, in the hope that their desire to hold on to their money may overpower their craving for the cigarette.

In the same way, fine yourself if you lose your temper. Your desire not to lose money will make you more vigilant.

> *Rav Yehudah Tzadkah would always warn his students to put seven locks on their mouths. The Rosh Yeshivah asked his students to pay a one* lira *penalty each time they spoke* lashon hara.
>
> *One day one of his students was overheard speaking* lashon hara. *His friends reprimanded him, but he was convinced that they were wrong. He ended up repeating his words eight times. When the Rosh Ye-*

shivah was informed of the comments, he asked the boy for eight liros.

On another occasion the Rosh Yeshivah placed a lira on the table and claimed to have stumbled in this area. No one believed him.

(Ve'zos Le'Yehudah)

The Right Environment

When asked by his teacher, Rabi Yochanan ben Zakai, what good path to take in life, Rabi Yossi replied, "[having] a good neighbor" (*Pirkei Avos* 2:9). The Rambam points out that we are greatly influenced by the people among whom we live. He advises that we stay far away from the wicked and cling to Torah Sages in order to learn from them and have their good character rub off on ours (*Mishneh Torah, Hilchos Deios* 5–6)

Find a social setting and environment that supports the character changes you want to make. Pick a Rav who is an *adam gadol*, a great man whose deeds will set the standards you seek to emulate. Consult with him whenever you are uncertain of the direction you should take.

The Alter of Slobodka once had the opportunity to speak in learning with a well-known genius. After a three-hour conversation he commented, "He has studied and reviewed, but hasn't served great men."

It was possible to detect an insufficiency in the man's service of Hashem because he had never merited serving great men and studying their ways.

Steer clear of friends who indulge. Don't associate with people who make you feel like a misfit for taking life seriously.

Socialize with people who have good character traits and know how to make the best of life's opportunities. If you know someone who excels at a certain trait, by all means try to discover the secrets of their success. The Piaseczne Rebbe recommends that we model ourselves after people who are experts at the trait we are trying to master. We need to observe how they conduct themselves — how they interact with their Creator, their families, and their friends. Use them as a basis for comparison to gauge your own accomplishment as you scale the heights of that character attribute. If possible, approach these people and ask for guidance.

When working on self-improvement it is helpful to create circumstances where we are forced to perform.

> *Rav Dovid Povarsky recounted that in Kelm, when a person had difficulty davening well without distracting thoughts, he would undertake to be the sh-liach tzibbur. Davening on behalf of the minyan would ensure that the* tefillah *was a good one. Self-consciousness would force the individual to daven well.*
> (*Mussar Ve'daas*, Part II, *Maamar* 27)

If it is hard for you to daven with concentration, try sitting next to the Rav, or near people who are focused on their prayers. If you find it difficult to make a commitment to learn, offering to give a *shiur* will force you to prepare. Do you have a hard time giving charity? Give it in a public setting so you receive honor for it.

Mitzvos are designed to break our egocentricity and force a confrontation with our weaknesses. The fortunate among us have the constant support and guidance of parents, family, and friends, who expect the highest standards from us. We are constantly exposed to examples of people whose lives and characters reflect the battle to improve themselves. We work on developing a close relationship with a teacher or Rav who motivates us on a personal level to correct ourselves.

When Hashem sees us working to create an environment that helps us avoid sin, we merit help from Above (Vilna Gaon).

Letting Others Know

Communicate your determination to change. Talk about it to a spouse or a good friend. The ensuing embarrassment you would feel for not living up to your new standards may help you to stand up to your *yetzer hara*.

> *A woman shared the following story with me:*
>
> *Each summer, when her children were away at camp, she would allow herself certain indulgences that she admitted were spiritually detrimental. One summer she told her husband that this year, she had decided to give up that practice. She was determined to no longer frequent those places.*
>
> *Just as she finished letting him in on her resolution, the phone rang. It was the friend who usually accompanied her on these jaunts. She could not believe that her decision was being tested so quickly by such a tempting offer. Because her husband was*

sitting there, she found the strength to tell her friend of her determination not to go.

Now, five years later, she cannot imagine that there was a time when she enjoyed such indulgences.

Total Commitment

Rus and Orpa were both sisters and sisters-in-law. Although determined to stay with their mother-in-law after their spouses' deaths, ultimately only Rus stayed on, while Orpa turned her back on the Jewish People.

Rus demonstrated her devotion to her mother-in-law and to the Jewish People, and is rewarded by being granted the privilege of becoming the progenitor of the House of David. Orpa, on the other hand, sank into degeneracy that very night. One sister rises to the highest summit, while the other descends to the lowest nadir. How is it possible for the change to occur so quickly?

There is no middle ground in the service of Hashem. A person who thinks that he can make concessions to the *yetzer hara* and still maintain his spiritual growth is making a grave error.

The *Gemara* informs us: "Satisfy it and it becomes ravenous; starve it, and it becomes satiated" (*Sanhedrin* 107a). It is dangerous to rationalize and say, "I will give in to the *yetzer hara* just this once and then its magnetic allure will slacken. On the contrary by giving in to temptation once, it becomes stronger next time rather than weaker. "The only proven remedy is to heal the hunger [of the *yetzer hara*] through hunger itself" (*Michtav Me'Eliyahu*, Vol. 1, page 46)

> *It can be compared to a person who is straddling the windowsill on the eighth floor of an apartment building. People below scream up to him, "Have you gone crazy? Do you want to end your life?"*
>
> *With a relaxed smile on his face, he responds, "No, of course not! I am just going to jump down to the fifth floor — I'm not going any further than that."*

The man is a fool. He lacks a basic understanding of the laws of physics. And the same principle applies in the spiritual arena. One who continuously works to scale the mountain of Hashem's service will be able to retain his standing. But once he slides down, even a small beginning can lead to a free fall, resulting in a total spiritual breakdown.

The Torah discusses just two alternatives: walking in Hashem's ways or rejecting Hashem's Torah, with the associated blessings or curses (*Vayikra* 26:3–16). What about the intermediate path — the person who doesn't keep the mitzvos as they should be kept, but certainly does not deny the Torah's binding authenticity?

The Torah does not describe this option because this path does not truly exist. The moment a person abandons his striving to fulfill the word of Hashem, he has embarked on the path to denial. There is no alternate course. We must proceed with conscious awareness of this principle, to avoid Orpah's fate of being reduced to wickedness — without fully understanding how we ever fell so low.

Using Imagination For Personal Growth

The *yetzer hara* uses the imagination to encourage us to satisfy our selfish desires. Yet in our attempts to resist the blandishments of the *yetzer hara* and mold the selfish tendencies of "a wild ass" into a *"mentsch"* (*Alter of Kelm on Iyov* 11:12), the imagination can be an important tool for change.

It is our ability to imagine that enables us to transcend reality as we perceive it, and open up new possibilities for creative spiritual growth. What our imagination conjures up becomes alive in our eyes. Imagination can make a person feel that he is actually in a situation that only his imagination has placed him in.

The *yetzer hara* uses imagination as a tool to convince us that illusion is actually reality. For example, someone wants to stay up late. In his imagination, he's convinced that staying up late won't do any harm. And so what if he's tired or irritable as a result? He'll still be able to function! Under the skillful guidance of the *yetzer hara*, imagination can supplant common sense.

It is valuable to note that indulgence of the senses is the most powerful of drives. The desires of this world draw a person like a magnet. The best way to overcome one's negative impulses is to be aware of how illusory these pleasures actually are. As soon as you take a closer look with your intellect, you will see how empty and meaningless it is. As soon as you start asking questions to clarify the reality of the *yetzer hara*, you will find that there is nothing there. This is analogous to seeing a shadow and thinking that something is actually there. As soon as you light a candle, you realize that what you saw was only an illusion. Use your intellect to see the emptiness of negative desires and you will be free of their pull. (*Ohr Yahel*, Vol. 2, page 35)

Stand up to the *yetzer hara* by using its tactics: replace the *yetzer hara* imaginings with those of the *yetzer tov*.

He was known as the "Old Kohein" or sometimes the "Russian Melamed.*" Even when Rav Mordechai Leib Kaminsky was an old man he was up each evening at one in the morning. By two he was in the* beis medrash. *Even those evenings when there was a curfew or bombs were flying overhead, nothing would prevent him from making his way to the* beis medrash.

One night, during the last days of the British Mandate, on his way to shul, Rav Mordechai Leib was stopped by a contingent of British soldiers. "Where are you going?" they called out. Although he knew no English he understood their intent and replied, "Synagogue," in his Belarusian accent. When their commander looked into his face, he perceived that Rav Mordechai Leib was a holy man. He ordered some soldiers to accompany him to his destination. So it was that an old Jew carrying a lantern was observed walking towards shul with several soldiers at his side.

He would say, "I am an old soldier. I must get up early. Don't think that age prevents me from sleeping; I would much prefer staying under my blanket but orders are orders."

*Whenever he woke up he would jump out of bed
and start learning until daybreak even if he had just
gone to bed only an hour before. He accounted for
this behavior by sharing an incident that happened
in his youth. He had been seriously ill and the doctors
had despaired of his life. Hashem willed otherwise
and he got better. When he was back on his feet, he
concluded that he really deserved to die but that
Hashem decided to put off the decree for later. He
then compared himself to the generation that had
been led out of Egypt and had been condemned to die
in the dessert because of their transgression. On the
night of Tishah Be'Av the men would enter the graves
they had dug and waited to see if Hashem would take
their souls. Many of the survivors undoubtedly fell
asleep but when they awoke to life they certainly
jumped up and ran joyously to their tents.*

*"That same feeling motivates my behavior when
I wake up and see that I am still alive. It is impossible for me to fall back asleep. I immediately leap out
of bed and learn until daybreak."*

*(Sippurim Yerushalmim, page 69; Sheal Avicha
Ve'yagedcha, Part II, page 293)*

Supplant the thoughts of the *yetzer hara* with the
thoughts of the *yetzer tov*. If you see something forbidden
in the street, focus your mind inward and review the *gemara* you are presently studying. If your mind strays during
davening, don't think, "I have to get rid of these thoughts
and focus." Instead, use your imagination to conjure up the

reality of the *Beis Ha'mikdash*, with the angels surrounding you in response to your heartfelt prayers.

INSPIRATION

The wicked are controlled by their desires and the righteous are in control of their desires (*Bereishis Rabbah* 67:8).

The *Kuzari* describes the ultimate pious individual as a man who establishes harmony between his physical and intellectual faculties, and with his willpower directs them to obey and serve him. He directs his memory to retain the visions of spiritual scenes and guards against imaginings that confuse the truth and cause doubt.

(*Kuzari*, Gate III, page 1)

Rav Simcha Zissel of Kelm asked the question we often ask — how did our forefathers and the great tzaddikim we read about reach the heights that they did? His answer? They knew how to manipulate their imagination to beat the *yetzer hara* at its own game. They lived with a clear vision of the spiritual realities of their existence, with the ability to staunchly dedicate their imagination to submission and service of Hashem.

This is a particularly powerful way of fighting negative thoughts and character lapses. For instance, an individual who wants to share a juicy piece of *lashon hara* with a friend should picture the person he wants to speak about begging him not to destroy his reputation. In another example, someone who needs to diet for his health and is tempted by an ice cream sundae, should try to vividly imagine himself lying on an operating table, with a surgeon reaching for a scalpel to make an incision in his chest. He may be able to leave the kitchen without the tempting treat.

Transform Abstract Concepts Into Vivid Images

The workings of the *yetzer hara* are so real, and the concept of the World to Come is so amorphous, that it is all too easy to lose sight of the really important focus of our lives. Rabbi Dessler notes that transforming abstract concepts into vivid images helps make these amorphous concepts relevant. The imagination can conjure images to inspire us to long for spiritual matters and make us enthusiastic about mitzvos.

Imagining Eternity

Grab a fistful of sand. Imagine that you were given the task of transferring one grain a day to another location. How long would it take to empty your hand? A good estimate would be about a year. What if you went to the beach and visualized moving the sand, grain by grain, to another location? How long would that take? Even if you were given countless of lifetimes to move the entire Atlantic coastline to the Pacific side, particle by particle, you would not be approaching the concept of eternity.

Eyes and Ears

Recall the *mishnah* in *Avos* (2:1): "An eye sees, an ear hears, and all your deeds are recorded in a book." When you are tempted by sin, visualize a big eye observing you; when you begin speaking *lashon hara*, see yourself speaking into a giant ear. Imagine someone sitting in a car and driving through the streets of your neighborhood, calling out the details of your transgressions over a microphone for all passersby to hear.

Public Video

Imagine viewing the video of your life with your friends and family seated beside you. Watch as the narrator reveals your innermost thoughts to all the spectators. Meditate deeply on these pictures. Try to visualize the shame of a naked soul, without the ability to rationalize, standing in the presence of Hashem. (Rabbeinu Yonah on *Avos*)

The Day of Death

"What man is he that lives, and will not see death, that will rescue his soul from the grasp of the grave" (*Tehillim* 89:49). If a person could keep in mind the day of his death, he would be saved from the *yetzer hara*. (*Berachos* 5b)

But the *yetzer hara* doesn't let us reflect on that. He encourages us to think the world is ours forever, and we will remain here indefinitely. (*Zohar*, Part III, page 126) Even those living with the infirmities of old age continue to live as if they are here to stay (*Michtav Me'Eliyahu* IV, pages 251–255).

People convince themselves that just as there is a group of people who learn *mishnayos*, and a group of people who gather to study *Shas* or *Ein Yaakov*, there is a group of people who are subject to death. "But not I!" each person thinks. "I haven't joined that group — I belong to the group of those who live!" (Chofetz Chaim)

• •

EXERCISE

How real is death to you? Do you live as if one day you will really die?

Tell your *yetzer hara* that after 120 years, your reception in the World to Come will not be very good if you don't make the effort now.

• •

Our Sages were good at this type of visualization.

> *The Sanzer Rav always went to the* mikveh *alone. A chassid who was himself a Rav wanted to observe the Rebbe, so he carefully hid inside the* mikveh *before the Sanzer Rav appeared. From his hiding place he could hear the Rebbe state, "I am now taking on myself the four methods with which the* beis din *killed a sinner." The Sanzer Rav thereby sought atonement for himself and the Jewish community.*

INSPIRATION

Rav Levi bar Hama says in the name of Rav Shimon bar Lakish: "A man should always incite his good impulse to fight against the evil impulse. For it is written, 'Tremble and don't sin.' If he subdues it, it is well and good. If he has trouble, he should study the Torah. For it is written, 'Commune with your own heart.' If he still has more difficulties, he should recite the *Shema*. For it is also written, 'On your bed.' Should the negative impulse still affect him, let him remind himself of the day of death. As it says, 'And be still, Selah.'"

(*Berachos* 5a)

Visualize Dramatic Events

Imagine uplifting scenes from the Torah, such as the giving of the Torah at Sinai (*Kuzari*, Gate III, page 5). Consider an image of the *Beis Ha'mikdash* and its miraculous proportions. Visualize the encampments of the Mishkan, the Leviim and Yisraelim, the Fire Pillar and the Cloud Pillar, and other such inspirational scenes; derive religious inspiration through this contemplation. (*Ha'maspik Le'ovdei Hashem*, Chapter 12)

> *When the Chofetz Chaim reviewed the story of the plague of frogs, he laughed heartily as he visualized the frogs' invasion of the homes and bodies of the Egyptians.*
>
> *Because of his deafness, Rav Chaim Shmuelevitz would stand beside the person reading the Torah. The* baal korei *would hear Rav Chaim weep when he read the* parshah *about the sale of Yosef or the* haftorah *about Chanah and Peninah. In the* Musaf *of Yom Kippur, when the deaths of the Ten Martyrs was described, and on Tisha Be'Av when the* piyut *was said as part of* Kinos, *Rav Chaim's tears would pour forth.*
>
> (*Rav Chaim Shmuelevitz*, page 148)

Transfer Emotions

When experiencing an emotional high, transfer your emotions to matters of the spirit. When Yosef fell on Yaakov's neck at their momentous meeting, Yaakov reacted by reciting *Shema*; he transferred the joy he felt to his spiritual strivings and enhanced his prayers.

When you hear good news, recite a few verses of *Tehillim* or learn a page of *Gemara* while you still have the full intensity of your joyous feelings. After that, it's time to share the good news with others.

Imagining It First

Rav Dessler writes about preparing for spiritual and moral challenges by living them in our imagination before they happen. For example, before visiting a difficult relative, mentally prepare yourself to absorb the criticism without reacting. In your imagination, see her barbs bouncing off you and vanishing in a puff of smoke.

> *Rav Dessler builds on the story of Rabi Akiva's death* (Berachos 9a). *His students see him saying the* Shema *as the Romans cruelly torture him. They ask him, "Is this the extent we must go?" He answers, "All my life I troubled myself over when I will be able to fulfill the verse, 'With all of your soul' – [explained by the Sages to mean] even if He takes your soul."*
>
> *Rabi Akiva's students, Rabbi Dessler explains, wondered how he was able to be totally concerned with Hashem's Unity even under the cruel tortures of the Romans. Rabi Akiva explained that for his entire life he had imagined this moment. When it actually came, it was natural for him to actualize it.*

Envision yourself as the ideal, spiritual person you aspire to be. Try to picture the outcome of the goals you are trying to achieve. Consider the joys you felt standing up to your *yetzer hara* as you forged ahead and fulfilled a mitzvah despite the difficulties. The Piaseczne Rebbe recommends that we imagine the greatness of our soul and see how it shines in Hashem's garden as He comes to enjoy your company with His holy entourage. (*Bnei Machsavah Tovah*)

Life Experiences

> As the illegal boat neared the shore of Eretz Yisroel, the passengers were chagrined to find a British warship blocking their path. Before they knew what was happening, the Holocaust refugees had been taken prisoner by the British and were sent to Cyprus. Imagine their feelings as they gazed through the barbed wire fences toward Eretz Yisroel, the destination they yearned for. So near, yet utterly inaccessible!
>
> Now imagine, Rav Dessler says, after 120 years, reaching the gates of Paradise—and being turned back.

Rav Yisroel Salanter and the Chofetz Chaim took two events they experienced and converted them into lessons for themselves and us all:

> Rav Yisroel Salanter was returning home very late one night. As he walked through the dark alleyways, he suddenly noticed that a light was still burning in the home of the shoemaker. He knocked on the

door and entered the shoemaker's home.

"Why are you still sitting and working at such a late hour?" asked Rav Salanter.

"As long as the candle burns," replied the shoemaker, "it is still possible to repair."

These words made a great impression on Rav Salanter, and he repeated them on many occasions. "Do you hear?" Rav Salanter would ask. "As long as the candle burns, it is still possible to repair! As long as a person is alive and his soul is within him, he can still rectify his deeds."

He pondered the lesson of that image. "As long as the light of the neshamah burns within us, I will continue to labor in my service of Hashem."

One day a cow wandered into the Chofetz Chaim's kitchen, overturning a crate of potatoes and creating all sorts of havoc. The Rebbetzin was beside herself.

When the cow was finally escorted out, the Chofetz Chaim commented, "When a person knows that there are cows outside, he must be careful to keep the door closed. When someone leaves or enters, he needs to open the door and immediately close it.

"It is the same with our spirituality. The yetzer hara waits for our mouths to open so it can initiate damaging speech in the form of lashon hara, rechilus, lying, and mockery. Be careful to keep the mouth closed. If you have to say something, say it — but don't leave your mouth open any more than is necessary."

(Sichos Ha'Chofetz Chaim II, page 23)

The *maggidim* of yesteryear were outstanding in their ability to transform day-to-day events into life-altering material for their lectures. Consider Rav Shalom Schwadron's attempt to enhance our understanding of the historical encounter between Yosef and his brothers.

Rav Schwadron tells of his own experience on board a ship nearing the shore of Eretz Yisroel. As everybody was busy getting ready to disembark, he noticed a young fellow traveler from Romania walking back and forth on the deck not far from where he stood. The youth's eyes kept sweeping the crowd of friends and relatives waiting on the quay. Rav Shalom could tell that he was beside himself with excitement. After a while, having searched every corner of the dock, he leaned forward continuing to seek, apparently in vain. He was clearly beside himself with fiery emotion.

Suddenly there was a scream from the crowd. An elderly women pushing to the front lifted her hands shouting, "Moshe!" She began running toward the ship. Shoving aside the harbor police she raced up the gangplank. A heartrending cry rose from the deck right near Rav Schwadron – "Mama! Mama!" And she continued to race crying, "Moshe!"

Heedless of those around him, including the police, the youth ran toward her crying "Mama!"

The police officers did not intervene as the two ran toward each other. They seemed paralyzed by the emotion of the moment.

Mother and son reached each other and em-
braced. Then came the tears — a whole flood of tears.
The two wept emotionally as they hugged and cried.
The spectacle was so poignant that all the Jews pres-
ent wept along with them. Rav Shalom was no ex-
ception.

It was the meeting of a mother and son who had
not seen each other since the beginning of World
War II. She had left her son with a Romanian fami-
ly. The police did their best to help, allowing the two
to hold on to each other, even setting out chairs for
them to make sure the older woman did not collapse
with emotion. Someone was sent to get the young
man's suitcase and the pair was respectfully sent on
their way.

Rav Shalom asks that we try to employ the story of the
encounter at dockside to get a handle on the encounter between Yosef and his brothers. The verse informs us that Yosef "raised his voice and wept." The brothers were bereft of
speech in the agony of their shame. "But his brothers could
not answer him because they were disconcerted before him."
(*Bereishis* 45:2–3)

Although those present at the encounter at dockside soon
forgot about the incident, our Sages did not permit the emotions of Yosef's encounter to dissipate. They raised their
voices in a poignant cry reaching out through the generations. "Woe unto us on the Day of Judgment; woe unto us
for the rebuke Yosef gave his brothers, who were then unable to answer him. How much more so, when Hashem will

come and rebuke each one of us according to what we have been. Woe unto us, for the Day of Judgment!"

Yosef was the youngest among the *shevatim*, a man of flesh and blood, and yet when he rebuked his brothers they were unable to answer him. How much more so will we be unable to stand up to Hashem who is both Judge and Claimant while sitting on the Throne of Judgment and judging each one of us? When our Sages witnessed something of value they used the power of their imagination to stir their emotions and raise themselves and others to greater spiritual heights.

Our own life experiences can be harnessed for enriching our inner spiritual lives. Hashem communicates with us through our experiences. We are wise to take advantage of these opportunities by transforming them into tools for moral development.

> *While walking along the seaside, I saw a posted sign warning of riptides, with instructions on what to do to if someone was caught in one. Although the natural reaction would be to swim against the tide, in fact a person should swim out to the side. Sometimes, when the* yetzer hara *attempts to lure us into sin, the best advice is not to resist, but to get involved in a marginal matter that will enable us to walk away from temptation.*

Meditations For Spiritual Growth

Meditations are a useful adjunct to prayer. When one prays, he should have a clear image of the words (that is, the form of the letters) in his mind, and intend to increase the power of holiness through them. (*Nefesh Ha'Chaim*, Gate 2, Chapter 13) Associating images with words helps keep the mind focused.

> *For example when you say the words* "Bechol naf-shechah – *with all your soul," visualize someone with a knife at your back. When you say the words* "Bechol meodecha – *with all your possessions," see yourself leaving your front door in the year 1492, surrounded by jeering Spaniards driving you into exile.*

Meditations can also aid in acquiring good character. Formulate an image of yourself—flawed, full of shame, and dirtied with sin— standing before the Divine Court with the Pure and Holy King of Kings and all of His hosts. That should be enough to remove the last vestiges of arrogance. (*Mesilas Yesharim*, Chapter 23)

When no one is present to encourage you, create your support in your mind. For example, when you find yourself reciting *berachos* too quickly, picture your friend or *rebbi* standing at your side, listening. Having difficulty avoiding speaking during davening? Visualize your teacher sitting in the row behind you.

Praying For Assistance

As you begin working on your character traits, don't forget to ask for help in this monumental task! Daven for assistance for dealing with a negative character trait. (*Kav Ha'yashar, Chapter 23*) Request that Hashem help you sacquire positive character traits (*Ziporen Shamir 3:47*).

It is particularly appropriate to ask for humility, since humility is the superconductor of all other good character traits. Ask for both the trait of humility and the acceptance of humiliation with joy. This will help us achieve a measure of atonement for sins of anger and pride. (*Reishis Chochmah*)

> *The rabbi of Sidra studied in Radin in the yeshivah of the Chofetz Chaim. He noted that the Chofetz Chaim would often lock himself into the* beis medrash *for a brief period of time. In an attempt to discover what he was doing, he hid under one of the seats in the shul. At midnight the Chofetz Chaim appeared, opened the* aron, *and began to pray to Hashem to help him overcome the anger that he was struggling with.*
>
> (*Tenuas Ha'mussar*)

> *Rabbi Yehudah Tzadkah had a very beautiful voice and was often asked to lead the prayers. Before he began praying, he was overheard asking Hashem to help him avoid falling prey to pride.*
>
> (*Ve'zos Le'Yehudah*)

Never Give Up

Sometimes, after working on a character trait for a long time, you see no progress. You become disheartened and conclude that nothing has been accomplished. But don't underestimate the small improvements — the few times you held back and remained in control. They are all valuable!

Don't give up when confronted by challenges. The Torah demonstrates the importance of this principle by citing the difficulties encountered by Yitzchok when he tried to dig wells. He did not give up when his wells were filled up — he continued digging them, a second and even a third time. (*Ha'Chofetz Chaim Chayav U'pealav*, page 1212)

One of the most valuable tools in personal growth is the knowledge that we have an important task in this world — and Hashem is rooting for us.

Yetzer Hara: Friend or Foe?

Know Your Enemy

The *yetzer hara* has numerous identities. In his most familiar form, he is the aspect of our psyche that encourages us to go against Hashem's will. He stands besides us, attempting to lure us into sin. He reaches out to block us when we try to perform a mitzvah. As long as we live, the *yetzer hara* monitors access to our hearts, trying to prevent any moral reproof form entering. He is like a corrupt guard, standing at the entrance to the royal palace, who only permits those who cooperate with him to enter. (*Ohr Ha'Chaim, Devarim* 21:18) Because the *yetzer hara* has a phenomenal ability to pull the wool over our eyes, the earlier we make the effort to isolate and engage him, the better. (*Ruach Chaim*, Chapter 2, *mishnah* 1)

The *yetzer hara* and the *malach ha'maves* are one and the same (*Bava Basra* 16). He comes to take our souls, and then leads the prosecution after our deaths. He acts as our prosecutor even while we are alive, rising Above to testify against us.

The *yetzer hara* enticed Adam and Chavah to sin, convincing them that they could serve Hashem better if they brought obscurity or murkiness to the world, then struggled to attain clarity (*Michtav Me'Eliyahu*, Vol. 2). In the Heavenly Court, he accused Avrohom and Iyov of being less righteous than they seemed. When Avrohom took his son Yitzchok for the Akeidah, the *yetzer hara* actually tried to persuade Avrohom that the command to slaughter his son had not come from Hashem, but the *yetzer hara* himself (*Michtav Me'Eliyahu*, Vol. 4, page 238). He encouraged the distressed Jews to forge a golden calf by showing them a false image of Moshe's dead body, and he still continues to prosecute us to this day for the weakness that led the Jews to sin.

In addition to the internal *yetzer hara,* which operates from within our hearts, there is an external *yetzer hara*: the influence of the nations in our environment. According to the Vilna Gaon, the external *yetzer hara* can be more difficult to overcome than the internal one, because man is greatly influenced by his environment. The impact of the nations among whom we live is exceedingly detrimental to our spirituality.

Food For Thought

The *yetzer hara* is described as an "old and foolish king." He is a king. Everyone obeys him, and he has many messengers. He is an elder. He has been around a long time, and he holds fast to a person from his youth, remaining with him through his old age. And he is called a fool, for he is a maker of fools. Everyone falls into his trap, resulting in grief and devastation.

(*Koheles Rabbah* 4:13)

Nosson the prophet compares the *yetzer hara* first to a passing traveler, then to a visiting guest (*II Shmuel* 12:4). First he is a chance companion, then he appears more frequently, and finally he takes over completely.

Who Am I?

In order to understand how the *yetzer hara* operates, we must consider the choices that come into play when we must choose between two or more alternatives. When a person says, "I want something," there are thousands of influences that use that channel called "I." The "I" can beckon or push away; it can strengthen or weaken resolution. What is the essence behind the "I"?

Two main factors motivate a person's decisions. One is called *will*, or *desire*. The other is the sensation of emotions of *enjoyment* or *pain*. Desire instinctively avoids pain and seeks pleasure, and pleasure anchors will at its side. A person looks for those things in life that brings enjoyment, and tries to avoid that which causes pain.

The *yetzer hara* gets a head start by joining us at birth. When a person's life begins, his only satisfactions are from physical pleasure. An infant cries at the slightest physical discomfort, and is relaxed and calmed by comfort. This is the power of the *yetzer hara*, stirring within. (*Bereishis Rabbah* 34:10)

By contrast, the *yetzer tov* only truly joins us at adolescence. When it arrives, the *yetzer tov* must do battle with the evil inclination, which has already thrived within the person for a long time. As a person grows and matures, he develops himself spiritually, and begins to gain more satisfaction from spiritual than from physical gain. This indicates the maturity of the *yetzer tov*.

It is up to us to assist our *yetzer tov* as soon as it makes its appearance. The *yetzer hara's* influence can be compared to an insidious illness spreading silently from one part of the body to another, without the person's awareness of his body's struggle. (*Ohr Yechezkel*; *Ohr Le'tziyon*) Unless we seek to differentiate between the two voices that clash within us, our *yetzer hara* will inevitably retain his mastery over our inner self.

Rav Yisroel Perlow, the Yanuka of Stolin, was ordained as Rav at the tender age of thirteen. His first lecture to the assembled chassidim and guests was a masterful display of profound knowledge and deep understanding of all aspects of the Torah.

Before bentching on that great day, the elder chassidim asked their young Rebbe, "What did you tell the 'old and foolish king,' the yetzer hara, *when he tried for thirteen years to lure you away from performing the mitzvos?"*

The Yanuka replied, "I told that 'old and foolish king' to leave me alone. I pointed out to him that the Torah specifically prohibits a judge from making any ruling based on the evidence presented by only one side. Since I was not yet old enough to have the benefit of the advice of the 'good and wise king,' the yetzer tov, *I had not yet heard his side of the matter. Therefore, I was not permitted to judge solely on the word of the* yetzer hara. *I told him to wait until my bar mitzvah, when I gain the* yetzer tov *and would have the knowledge and protection of the mitzvos. Only then would I reply to his enticements."*

(*Men of Distinction*, page 195)

A person must constantly be alert to the blandishments and schemes of his *yetzer hara*. He must learn to think before he acts, analyzing a given situation to determine if it is the advice of the *yetzer tov* or *yetzer hara*. How puny is the mind overruled by desire, and how great the mind ruled by the soul! (*Iggeres Ha'mussar*)

Comprehension is the *yetzer tov*'s greatest tool. That is why he arrives at maturity. Having acquired insight, a person can persevere with his upward itinerary. Using his intelligence, which strives constantly for truth, he will be able to devise his own strategies to conquer the *yetzer hara*. (Toras Ha'bayis, Chapter 10)

The *yetzer tov* speaks in earnest tones, admonishing us to behave. The *yetzer hara*'s persuasions are of a different nature entirely. A person who dedicates himself to truth can distinguish the difference, separating white from black, good from bad, and reality from fabrication. If we draw on this G-d-given inner strength, ultimately we will be victorious.

Food For Thought

For the *yetzer tov* to assume control, enlighten all aspects of our body, and control our animal soul, a person must remain calm. When a person is distracted, his wisdom departs and the animal soul has nothing to rein it in. At those times, it is easy to get sidetracked. Good news, bad news, pain, stress, pleasure — any changes in our daily routine, and we lose our clarity. This weakens our *yetzer tov*, resulting in mistakes that will have to be rectified, thus wasting time.

(*Shevilim Be'machshavah Ha'chassidus*)

The *yetzer hara* manipulates us. We metamorphose from predator to pussycat at his behest. (*Shemiras Ha'lashon, Shaar Ha'Torah*, Chapter 6) We should seek to take the big challenges and break them down into smaller ones. It will then be easier for us to face up to the *yetzer hara*'s attempts to seduce us into sin.

Taking Time

Occasionally the *yetzer hara* moves so quickly that by the time we realize we have done something wrong, it is too late. Most of our sins are committed because we did not take the time to think matters through before putting thought into action. (*Madreigas Ha'adam*)

Every act, no matter how insignificant it may appear, must be examined through the prism of Torah, taking care to foresee all possible consequences.

The Brisker Rav never made a decision without looking into all the various aspects of the resolution.

On the way to Eretz Yisroel, the Brisker Rav was forced to stop in Odessa. He chose not to daven in the local shul that Shabbos. His fellow travelers wanted to understand the reason for his decision, wondering if they, too, should refrain from going to that shul.

The Brisker Rav explained that he was concerned that if he went to daven in the shul, the local Jews would hear of his arrival and want to ask him all kinds of questions. "There might be Soviet agents in the shul," he said, "and when they see the local people speaking with a foreign citizen, they may invent false accusations, and make arrests — or worse. And I am not prepared to be the cause of anyone's suffering!"

(*The Brisker Rav*, pages 497–498)

When the Chozeh of Lublin suspected that a thought stemmed from the *yetzer hara*, he would say, "Wait while I think about it, and I will see if I am ready to cooperate." The possibility of reflection discourages the *yetzer hara*, and he moves on to greener pastures. The *yetzer hara* functions best in a murky environment, when the situation remains cloudy and is not penetrated by the light of logic. (*Divrei Shmuel*)

For the *yetzer hara*, tomorrow does not exist. He wants everything *now*. "Tomorrow" is an intellectual concept, with built-in restraints. Because the *yetzer hara* refuses to be shackled, he says, "Listen to me *today*, and tomorrow you can begin working on yourself." You must reply, "*Today* I will not listen to you. Tomorrow — well, we'll see." (Slonimer Rebbe)

On one of his trips abroad Rav Shabsi Yudelevitch found himself seated next to a prominent Jewish zoologist.

To the horror of the Maggid, his seatmate received a nonkosher meal and eagerly began eating his portion. The Maggid turned to him and asked him how he could permit himself to consume such disgusting food.

The zoologist was quite insulted. "I am descended from a family of rabbis, yet I cannot see how I am obligated by what Moshe conveyed thousands of years ago!"

The Maggid trembled at those heretical words. "Was it Moshe Rabbeinu who said those words? They were said by Hashem, in the presence of the entire nation at Mount Sinai!"

"How do you know that?" challenged the zoologist. "If you can prove that to me I will do teshuvah. *In all fairness, however, I must warn you that many have tried, but no one has succeeded in demonstrating the Divine origin of the Torah to my satisfaction."*

The Maggid responded, "Because you are a zoologist, it should not take more than five minutes to offer you proof that I am sure you will appreciate."

The zoologist raised his brows in surprise. "I'm all ears," he said.

"You are probably aware," the Maggid began, "that two signs identify an animal as kosher: it must chew its cud and have split hooves."

The zoologist nodded.

"If an animal only chews its cud but does not have split hooves, or it has split hooves but does not chew its cud, that animal is not considered kosher," the Maggid continued.

His zoologist nodded his agreement again.

"The Torah actually specifies the four types have that have only one of these two signs: the camel, two types of rabbits, and the pig. The first three chew their cud, but do have split hooves. The pig has split hooves, but does not chew its cud."

"Yes," the zoologist said. "I know all this."

"Let me ask you a question," the Maggid said. "Why did the Torah need to list these exceptions by species? We would readily understand that if any animal does not fulfill the two required conditions, then they are automatically nonkosher."

"An excellent question," the zoologist agreed.

"Let me remind you that Moshe Rabbeinu never studied in any university," the Maggid continued. "He never had the opportunity to master the science of zoology. He never worked in a zoo, and was certainly was not a hunter by profession. His resume included shepherding in the desert and leading the Jewish People—professions that did not bring him into contact with the diverse animal species scattered throughout the world.

"So explain it to me," he pressed the zoologist. "Explain how Moshe Rabbeinu, living thousands of years ago, was able to cite the only four species in the entire globe who carry only one of the two signs *of kashrus! Remember that in those days, there were entire continents that remained unexplored. Some lands had never been seen by humans at all. Despite the fact that scientists have now catalogued millions of species in remote corners of the world, they have still not discovered even one animal with one of the two signs. If the Torah is not Divine, how is that possible?"*

"I don't know," the zoologist admitted.

The Maggid concluded, "The only logical explanation is that the Torah is of Divine origin, transmitted to Moshe Rabbeinu by Hashem, Who created everything in this world and is familiar with every species that exists. There is no other possibility!"

The zoologist looked awed. "Rebbi," he declared, "you win. I must now honor my commitment to do teshuvah, *for you have kept your part of the bargain!" Then, picking up his fork again, he added, "As soon as I finish eating, I will start ..."*

The yetzer hara *would not permit him to comply at that moment, convincing him to delay his* teshuvah *until a later time. But after the* treif *meal was consumed, the commitment was forgotten, and the man tragically remained unchanged as before.*

(*Derashos Ha'maggid, Moadim I, pages 12–15*)

Rather than allowing the *yetzer hara* to delay our fulfillment of mitzvos until some distant tomorrow, delay the *yetzer hara*'s demands instead!

Anyone on guard duty received a fur coat to protecting him against the bitter cold of the Russian nights. One frigid Friday night, it was the Steipler's turn to stand guard. The non-Jew who was sentry before him removed the fur coat and hung it on a sturdy branch, unaware that his Jewish fellow soldier would not be able to remove it from the branch on Shabbos.

Faced with the temptation of the coat and the biting cold, the Steipler said to himself, "For one minute I will manage without a coat." When the minute passed, he repeated the sentence again: "I can manage without the fur coat for one minute more." The Steipler passed the entire night in this fashion, delaying for one minute at a time, and thus avoided chillul Shabbos.

PRACTICAL ADVICE

- You wake up to a frosty cold morning. An inner voice says, "You feel sick. You coughed a few times yesterday, too. Rest a little more and see if you feel better." Is it the *yetzer hara* speaking? The best way to tell is to get up! Have a hot drink, move around, and then decide what to do.
- Feel a craving for something tempting? Wait five minutes and see if you are still hungry.
- Feeling tired? Tell the *yetzer hara* to give you fifteen minutes without any interruptions, and after that you will go to sleep. In fifteen minutes, try that line again.

A businessman hired a driver to take him to the fair. It was a warm summer day, and the swaying carriage soon rocked the businessman to sleep. Before long, the driver found his head nodding, and he too was sound asleep.

As soon as the horses realized that the reins were lax, they began drifting to the side of the road, stopping to nibble on plants that caught their attention. Then the horses spotted a lush patch of grass and galloped toward it, overturning the wagon in the process.

The driver and passenger found themselves rudely awakened.

"What happened?" the driver called out.

"What happened?" the businessman angrily snapped back. "The wagon turned over! Can't you see?"

"I will whip the horses," the driver said, trying to scramble to his feet.

"It is you who deserves a beating," the passenger declared. "You are the one at fault for letting go of the reins!"

"Me?" the driver protested. "I saw that the horses were proceeding down the road, and I assumed that they would continue as they should. Who would have imagined that they would abandon the path?"

The businessman was enraged. "You aren't making any sense! Horses are only animals. How can you rely on them to know the way? As long as they feel that the reins are held by a firm hand, they stay on course. But when the grip loosens, they do as they please."

Rav Moshe of Coucy explains that the body is like an animal and the soul like an angel. If the soul is in control, then all is well; but if the soul loosens its grip, then the body will throw its master into a ditch.

(*Shem Olam*, Chapter 18)

Food For Thought

Chazal describe the dangers of the *yetzer hara*: "The *yetzer hara* is terrible, for even its Creator calls it evil, as it says, 'For the inclination of a person's heart is bad from his youth'"

(*Bereishis* 8:21)

Rav Yitzchok says, "A person's *yetzer hara* renews itself against him every day, as it says, 'Only evil every day'"(*Bereishis* 6:5).

Rav Shimon ben Levi says, "A person's *yetzer hara* escalates every day and seeks to kill him, as it says, 'The wicked man watches for the *tzaddik* and seeks to kill him' (*Tehillim* 37:32). If Hashem would not help the person, he would not be able to overcome the *yetzer hara*, as it says, 'Hashem will not leave him in his hands' (ibid, 37:33)."

(*Kiddushin* 30b)

The *yetzer hara* is called *enemy*, because he seeks any means at his disposal to trap us and defeat us.

(*Succah* 52a)

How much power does the *yetzer hara* have? Reb Chiya compares him to dough, maintaining that corruption is inherent in our nature. Abba Yosef compares the *yetzer hara* to leaven, suggesting that the dough is generally untainted, but is corrupted by contact with him. The Sages compare him to a lowly plant, implying that human beings are not corrupt by nature; we are basically good, even though we might be swayed by the *yetzer hara*'s wiles.

(*Bereishis Rabbah* 34:10)

A young person struggles with the temptations of youth, and an older person deals with those of an adult. The *yetzer hara* has inducements for every person, at any age. He operates like a real estate broker, closing the big deals even as he keeps an eye on the smaller transactions. That is why a person must still struggle with his *yetzer hara*, even when he grows older. (*Ohr Yechezkel*)

Rav Yitzchok Isaac Rot, a Klausenberger chassid, was a Holocaust survivor who became a shochet *in Eretz Yisroel. When he retired, he sat in the* beis medrash *full time, learning and teaching. He gave lectures in* Shulchan Aruch – Yoreh Deah, *and* Zohar. *His rigorous schedule began at dawn, even in his old age.*

A young man discovered him crying in the beis medrash *early one morning. Fearing for Rav Isaac's
health — he was then over ninety years old — the young
man rushed to his side, asking him what was wrong.*

Rav Isaac moaned, "I thought that I had my
yetzer hara *under control, but this morning I saw
otherwise ..."*

"What happened?" asked the young man.

*The elderly Klausenberger chassid answered,
"Every morning, I rise like a lion to get out of my bed
while it is still dark. Today my* yetzer hara *tried to
stop me."*

*The young man was bewildered. "But I see you
are here, as always."*

Rav Isaac began to weep. "Isn't it enough that my
yetzer hara *is still trying to stop me from going to the*
beis medrash? *Do you want me to listen to him as
well?"*

(*Borchi Nafshi*, pages 269–270)

Tactics Of The *Yetzer Hara*

The *Mesilas Yesharim* explains how the *yetzer hara*
works. He hides the sin, as it says, "You make darkness and
it is night" (*Tehillim* 104:20). This leads to mistakes, as it
says, "The simpletons keep going and are punished" (*Mishlei*
22:3). The *yetzer hara* prevents him from discerning what is
substantial and what is trivial. (*Bava Metzia* 83b)

The *yetzer hara* tries to convince us to busy ourselves with
the issues of others, instead of improving ourselves. We worry
about our friends who are not compassionate, our relatives

who are spending too much money, or our neighbors who talk too much *lashon hara*. We must remind ourselves that the *Mishnah* describes the person being in control of *his yetzer hara*, and not those of others. We must allow other people to struggle with their *yetzer hara*, and concentrate our energies on our own temptations. (Rav Naftali of Ropshitz)

The *yetzer hara* attacks at whatever level is most likely to achieve success. He speaks to us in a seductive manner, using words that sound like our words and a voice that sounds like our voice. He attempts to entice us to sin in the most appealing modes, mirroring precisely the spirit of the day and adjusting his arguments to our train of thought. Each situation comes with its own set of beguiling temptations.

When the *yetzer hara* takes action to block our way, he adjusts his tactics to suit the moment. For example, he can contrive numerous rationales to ensure that a girl doesn't help her mother. On one occasion, he takes advantage of her tiredness and convinces her that she will be able to help more properly after a quick, restoring nap. The next thing she knows, it is morning, and her mother has done the job herself. The next evening, he makes her feel so overwhelmed by homework that she arranges for a sibling to help her mother instead. An important *chesed* will require her attention for the next two nights, and everyone knows that a person doing one mitzvah is not obligated to lay it aside for another mitzvah. In this fashion, the *yetzer hara* manages to prevent this girl from helping her mother all week long. (Based on a discussion in Bais Yaakov High School of Boro Park, Class M7, 2008–2009)

The *yetzer hara* turns our *middos* against us. When a person has a chance to do a mitzvah, or impact the mitzvah performance of others, the *yetzer hara* stresses humility: "You are so insignificant." "No one will listen to you." "Better to show how modest you are, instead of telling others what to do." But if that same person is slighted or insulted, the *yetzer hara* will indignantly impel him to defend his honor, and wage war against those who offended him!

* *

Exercise

Life has been compared to walking up a down escalator. If one doesn't resolutely head upward, then one will inevitably move downward.

Visualize Yaakov's ladder with its foot on the ground and its head inclined heavenward. Each time you stand up to your *yetzer hara*, you climb up a rung. Each time you give in to his blandishments, you retreat down a rung.

(*Zachor Le'Miriam*, Chapter 13)

* *

The *yetzer hara* has many guises and tools in his arsenal. Recognizing his different aspects and manifestations can help us recognize and defeat him.

Mitzvah Or Not?

The *yetzer hara* may try to convince us that the mitzvah we are about to perform is actually a transgression. If we are unsure of the source of a thought, consider where that thought will lead us. If the suggestion results in delay or denial of action, it is certainly the advice of the *yetzer hara*. Will it lead to positive, factual good, or will it result in no activity at all?

If there is a choice between two different mitzvos, the *yetzer hara* will try his best to convince us to do neither. But if the result is that one of those mitzvos — or, even better, both of them — will be performed, then we can rest assured that the inspiration comes from the *yetzer tov*.

Rav Nochum of Chernobyl once received a gift of three hundred rubles. The gabbai *was overjoyed, for now the Rebbe would finally be able to pay off some of the household debts. He sat down to prepare a list of all the creditors and calculate how much he would be able to give each of them in partial payment.*

When the Rebbe finished receiving his petitioners, the gabbai *entered the Rebbe's study to receive the long-awaited money. The* tzaddik *opened his drawer and told the* gabbai *to help himself. The* gabbai *peered into the drawer and could only stare in stunned silence. There were only a few small coins left.*

The tzaddik, *seeing the* gabbai's *shock, asked him gently, "Why do you look so sad? Has the One Who provides bread for all creatures not shown us, in His loving-kindness, undeserved generosity?"*

The gabbai, *who agonized over the debts and privation that hung over the Rebbe's household, could no longer restrain himself. "But what of are the three hundred rubles that chassid brought?" he protested. "That sum could have helped us pay off some of our debts!"*

The Chernobyler Rebbe patiently explained that soon after he received the gift, a chassid appealed to

him for financial assistance. He had not paid the vil-
lage melamed *for his children's tuition for an entire*
year; the local squire had threatened to drive him
out of his house because of his arrears on the rental
of the millstones; and he had to arrange a wedding
for his eldest daughter.

The Rebbe continued, "I felt that Hashem wanted
to give me the special privilege of being the agent for
the disbursement of charity in a way that would
earn me three mitzvos at once. I asked the chassid
how much he needed, and he said, 'Three hundred
rubles.' Then and there, I decided to give him the en-
tire amount I had received.

"But then another thought came to mind. An
amount such as this could bring relief to numerous
poor families, not just one lucky recipient. This
seemed only proper, and I could not decide which
thought was the right one.

"After weighing the two arguments, I concluded that
the voice that proposed dividing up the amount for sev-
eral families did not come from the yetzer tov *at all.*
How did I know that? Because if this had been the view
of the yetzer tov, *then as soon as the money was given*
to me, the yetzer tov *would have immediately said, 'Na-*
chum, here. Take the three hundred rubles and divide it
up into six parts. Give away five parts to the needy, and
keep one for yourself.' But he did not say that. It was
only after Hashem offered me the privilege of helping
this poor chassid that this voice came along and made
such a cunning suggestion!

"It could only have been the yetzer hara *speaking, and I resolved to reject him. I took the advice of the* yetzer tov *instead—I called back that poor fellow and gave him the whole amount."*

(A Treasury of Chassidic Tales, Vol. II, pages 532–534)

The Chofetz Chaim once visited a certain city before Yom Kippur. As was his wont, he asked the Rav if there were any deeds that required improvement that he might seek to address. The Rav explained that there was one disturbing custom that he could not uproot from the community: they rushed through the Neilah *prayer so they could hurry home and break their fast. He had tried many times to rebuke them, but without success. The people claimed that the custom had precedence over halachic requirements, particularly when it was a matter of life and death.*

The Chofetz Chaim asked the Rav to inform the community that he would be speaking on Shabbos. The people crowded into shul to listen, and the Chofetz Chaim walked to the podium and began to speak.

"The yetzer hara *is often called a thief. Why do we engage in this uncomplimentary name-calling? After all, the* yetzer hara *is a hard worker, fulfilling his mission with dedication and zeal. If anyone deserves disapproval, it is we who are influenced by his urgings to behave in an unseemly manner!*

"With your permission," the Chofetz Chaim continued, "I would like to tell you a story.

"There was a Jew who just couldn't earn enough to support his family. Out of desperation, he decided to do something illegal and potentially dangerous. He smuggled himself across the border and purchased a large quantity of luxurious fabric for an inexpensive price. He crossed back into the country and headed towards the nearest city, keeping to the woods and avoiding the well-traveled roads. As he neared his destination, his heavy pack on his back, he dreamed of the hefty amount he would receive when he sold the goods.

"Suddenly, he heard footsteps behind him. He almost stopped breathing as a border guard appeared at his side. He thought of running, but the heavy bolts of fabric would slow him down, and if he threw away his pack, he would lose a fortune.

"He decided that his only available option was to act innocent. He warmly greeted the policeman, who replied in kind.

"The Jew, still trying to act like an innocent traveler, said to the policeman, 'I am so happy to have met you! It is good to have company when you are on the road.'

"The policeman was equally gracious. 'My joy is no less than yours at having someone to accompany me,' he declared, and the two of them walked along the road, conversing companionably.

"When they arrived at the city gates, the policeman

turned to the Jew and said, 'Please come with me.'

"*Nervously, the Jew asked, 'Where?'*

"*The policeman replied, 'To the police station, of course. You are carrying illegal goods on your shoulder. The fabric will be confiscated and you will be brought to trial for your crime.'*

"*The Jew stared furiously at the policeman and hissed, 'Thief!'*

"*The policeman was offended by the Jew's accusation. 'Why are you insulting me?' he demanded. 'You are trying to earn a living and so am I. You engage in illegal activities, and you find fault with my behavior?'*

"*The unfortunate Jew retorted, 'I am not blaming you for my capture or for confiscating my goods and bringing me to justice. That is your job and I can't reproach you for that. But I am angry at you for pretending that you are my friend, and allowing me to carry the heavy load on my shoulder all these hours. If you had immediately informed me that I was your prisoner, I would have thrown down the heavy bolts of fabric. If you wanted the fabric, you could have carried it to the city yourself. You are a thief for deceiving me.'*"

The Chofetz Chaim concluded: "*Now you can understand why the* yetzer hara *is called a thief. If he were to try to persuade us to eat and drink on Yom Kippur morning, we would certainly not listen to him! So he starts by recommending that we fast and pray. But when the day is nearly over, and we are already exhausted, then he persuades us to daven* Neilah *early and eat a few minutes before the fast is actually over. This is how he steals the fast from us at the end of the day."*

At that moment, the members of that congregation resolved that from then on, they would complete the fast of Yom Kippur to the very end.

(*Kol Ha'Shabbos*, Elul 5719)

Food For Thought

"People think that the evil inclination looks like a murderer, a cross in one hand and an ax in the other, shouting at us, 'Kneel!' In fact, the *yetzer hara* is dressed in fine, white clothes and wrapped in silk. In one hand it holds a large, holy text, and in the other hand, sweet treats."

(Kotzker Rebbe)

Step By Step

Determining the *yetzer hara*'s ultimate goal can be tricky. When he approaches us dressed in fine, white clothes, he is difficult to identify. He will contrive "mitzvos" to make the individual stumble into a sin, or he will seek to trap the person into an insignificant sin by convincing the sinner that Hashem will forgive his minor infraction.

The *yetzer hara* often leads a person to sinfulness by degrees. A person who no longer comes to shul for Shacharis does not suddenly decide one fine day that davening is no longer for him. First, the *yetzer hara* convinces him that saying *Shema* by the time designated by the Magen Avrohom is not a requirement, but merely a stringency. With the passage of time, he barely says *Shema* by the time designated by the Vilna Gaon. Because he is now rising so late, he is left with too little time to put on tefillin. He reviews the halachic requirements and determines that saying the blessings before *Kriyas Shema* is not really a requirement. Soon, he gets used to sleeping until the last possible time for *Shema*. Getting to shul becomes more and more difficult, and after checking the sources, he concludes that davening on time is more important than davening in shul.

When you feel the *yetzer hara* trying to negotiate with you, run as fast as you can! Once a person is already engaged in the negative act, the *yetzer hara* throws all his arsenal into seducing him into continuing with the sin.

It is best to avoid the *yetzer hara* completely. Don't give in to him, even on small things. It is delusional to believe that a small *aveirah* won't really impact our relationship with Hashem. (Rebbe Rashab, *Kuntres Ha'mayaan*)

Too Difficult

The *yetzer hara* can deceive us into believing that even an easy commandment is extremely difficult. It is so challenging, in fact, that Hashem doesn't really expect us to perform it. The *yetzer hara* then persuades us that we will never achieve perfection anyway, so we shouldn't be overly distressed at adding this impossibly demanding transgression to our tally.

The Wrong Direction

The *yetzer hara* may allow you to identify an act as sinful, and guide you down another, apparently innocent route. But be cautious, for you may one day discover that this second choice was actually the sinful route that the *yetzer hara* wished you to follow in the first place.

> *A dog craves a loaf of bread. Crawling over to the baker's stand, he pretends to curl up and go to sleep. When the baker lowers his guard, the dog leaps up and overturns the stand.*
>
> *"Oh, no!" the baker cries. "The dog will steal all my bread!"*
>
> *The baker feverishly gathers all the loaves, and the dog seizes a single loaf of bread in its teeth and runs off.*
>
> *The baker, triumphant, announces to anyone listening, "I outsmarted that dog! It tried to steal all my bread, but I managed to stop it! It only escaped with a single loaf."*
>
> *In truth, it was the dog who outsmarted the baker, for it only wanted a single loaf of bread in the first place.*
>
> *(Bereishis Rabbah)*

> *A man crossed the border with two sacks tied to his bicycle.*
>
> *"What do you have in those sacks?" the border guard asked him.*

"Sand," the cyclist replied.

The skeptical guard did not believe him and inspected the sacks himself. When he saw that they indeed contained only sand, he let the cyclist past.

This scene repeated itself daily for months. At one point, the border guard even sent a sample of the sand to be analyzed. He could not believe that someone would go to all the trouble of lugging sand across the border. Yet he could never find any proof that the man was carrying anything other than ordinary sand.

Years later, the two met in a coffee house. The former border guard turned to the erstwhile cyclist and said, "Now you can tell me what you were smuggling. After all, I am retired, and the border between the two countries no longer exists."

The cyclist smiled and replied, "You thought I was smuggling sand. Actually, I was smuggling bicycles."

In the same fashion, the *yetzer hara* will try to get us to lower our guard. He will allow us to buy the long skirt instead of the short one, making us feel good about ourselves ... and convince us to ignore the fact that the long skirt is also too tight to be modest. He will not stop you from arranging a daily *shiur*, but he will make sure you choose the biggest talker in town as your learning partner. The *yetzer hara* does not prevent you from organizing an important event for charity or education, because he knows that you will neglect your family to keep it going. At the end of our lives, we may discover that the *yetzer hara* has deceived us in ways we never dreamed possible.

Insisting on Perfection

The *yetzer hara* may say to us, "A mitzvah only has value if it is done completely for Hashem's sake." He will coax us into such time-consuming preparations for a specific mitzvah that we are unable to perform the mitzvah as the Torah requires. Our holy thoughts will become profane, as our acts do not fulfill the letter of the law.

Consider the example cited by Rav Chaim Volozhiner: A person devotes his entire *Seder* trying to perfect the devotions associated with the eating of matzoh. As he strives to refine his sentiments, the hours pass in elevated reflection — until it is after daybreak.

The eating of matzoh at that time is rejected by Hashem. But a person who eats the matzoh on time has fulfilled the mitzvah, even if his chewing is not accompanied by the most elevated and devotional thoughts. (*Nefesh Ha'Chaim*, Gate 4)

Dressing Up Desires

When the *yetzer hara* wants to persuade you to indulge, he exaggerates the importance of the object of desire. You *must* have it, for you have never had anything like it! He causes a fever of excitement about this gadget, that outfit, a piece of jewelry, or new furnishings, until you can think of nothing else.

The *yetzer hara* may tempt our curiosity. He will arrange for us to be intrigued by the thought of a forbidden act or object, then feed that interest to maddening levels, until we long to personally experience what it would be like to try it.

The Baal Shem Tov suggests that we learn from the *yetzer hara*'s enthusiasm. Once he has succeeding in stoking your desire, the *yetzer hara* adds, "Hashem doesn't expect you to be able to overcome this type of challenge!" Learn from the *yezer ha'ra*'s dedication to his task—retain your devotion to Hashem, and refuse to listen. (*Ohr Ha'chochmah, Parshas Mikeitz*)

What's the Problem?

The *yetzer hara* can try to tempt us by reducing our comprehension of the potential transgression. "How can it be a problem if it's *glatt kosher*?" When we are close to succumbing, he may add, "How terrible could the punishment be?"

Food For Thought

Don't focus on the insignificance of the sin, but on the greatness of Hashem, Whose will we must obey.

(Rabbeinu Yonah)

Another favorite tactic of the *yetzer hara* is the inducement to try something *just once*. "Go ahead, try it. You're not going to do it more than once. Everyone's entitled to see what it's like." One puff, one click, one glance—and you are his.

I Deserve It

There's another tactic that might seem all too familiar: "You poor thing! You work so hard, and you're not even appreciated. You deserve the vacation, the summer home, the new car." Even if you have to beg, borrow, or steal, G-d forbid, the *yetzer hara* will make sure you want it, and get it.

"Why are you getting up so early?" the yetzer hara *asked the Ropshitzer Rebbe. "It's still dark outside! The stars are still visible in the sky!"*

The Rebbe laughed and replied, "You are up and around, and you are telling me to stay in bed?"

Destroying Mitzvos

If the *yetzer hara* cannot lead us to actual sin, then he injects his poison into our mitzvah performance. Laziness, regret, sometimes even despair over our performance of mitzvos — all this saps our mitzvos of their importance, and the reward dissipates. (*Kiddushin* 40b; *Toras Ha'bayis* 13)

> *The Chofetz Chaim had a granddaughter whom he loved dearly. Shortly before her wedding, however, she suddenly became ill and passed away. The family's joy turned into intense grief.*
>
> *At the time of his granddaughter's death, the Chofetz Chaim was about to publish another volume of the* Mishnah Berurah. *He was overheard saying to himself, "Satan! Satan! I know exactly what you're trying to do. You want me to be so depressed that I won't be able to finish the rest of the* Mishnah Berurah. *But let me tell you once and for all that you will never succeed! No matter what you do, I'll finish it."*
>
> (*The Rosh Yeshivah Remembers*, page 175)

Perhaps the *yetzer tov* has succeeded in convincing us to give *tzedakah*? The *yetzer hara* will try to persuade us that we needn't give quite so much, or that it would be better to give our generosity some publicity. (*Nefesh Ha'Chaim.* Gate 1, Chapter 6) Sometimes, he distracts us from focusing on the mitzvah, or allows us to serve Hashem, but for the wrong reasons or intentions. (*Sichos Ha'Chofetz Chaim* II, page 49)

Food For Thought

- You have some extra time on your hands, and you would like to learn. The *yetzer hara* persuades you that since you don't have the time to learn properly, you shouldn't try to learn at all.

- You start davening and can't muster proper concentration. Perhaps saying the words aloud in a powerful manner will help? The *yetzer hara* steps in and advises you that praying in such a seemingly pious manner would be two-faced.

- Your friend borrows your pen without permission, and you waste a lot of time looking for it. A few days later, you need a pen and you see his lying on his desk. Your *yetzer hara* says, "Take it. You will be teaching him a lesson he needs to learn."

- Your friend approaches you in shul after davening and starts a conversation. Your *yetzer hara* convinces you to reply, so he is not embarrassed in front of other friends who are standing nearby.

- The *yetzer hara* persuades you to learn during the *chazzan*'s repetition of Shemoneh Esrei.

- While saying *berachos*, your *yetzer hara* commends you for gathering the *seforim* and returning them to the shelves.
- The *yetzer hara* persuades you that refusing to shake hands with your client of the opposite sex will only cause a *chillul Hashem*.

The Chofetz Chaim would extinguish the lights in the beis medrash *each evening at ten o'clock, insisting that the boys all go to sleep. He informed his students that when the* yetzer hara *arrived in Radin, he was incapable of persuading the upright students not to learn. Knowing they would not listen to any attempts to persuade them to slacken their learning, the* yetzer hara *instead prompted the young men to stay up all night in pursuit of their Torah studies. What were the results? The students, with their weakened constitutions, became sick. The local doctors in Radin couldn't help, so the ill students were sent to Warsaw ... and there, the* yetzer hara *knows well what to do.*

When one of the boys studying in Radin took ill, the doctor ordered him to spend a month in a spa, where he would inhale the invigorating air and eat strengthening foods. The boy resisted the idea, finding it difficult to separate from the yeshivah and his friends, the Torah lectures, and prayers with a minyan.

The Chofetz Chaim observed that every day, we ask Hashem to remove the Satan from before and after us. It is easy to recognize the danger of the Satan

before us, for we confront him before every mitzvah.
He provides us with pious excuses for not doing what
we should, and tempts us to do what we should not.
But what is the danger of the Satan behind us, when
we have already defeated him?

When the yetzer hara *sees that we insist on fulfill-*
ing the mitzvos despite his blandishments, he steels up
behind us and gets involved in our mitzvah perfor-
mance. He suggests, "Learn nonstop and don't take
the time to eat or sleep, for every moment is precious."
A person listens to him and learns until he is incapa-
ble of functioning, and thus the yetzer hara *achieves*
his victory by corrupt means. He succeeds in leading
the students away from their goals. We must be care-
ful to examine each deed to see from where it stems.

(*Mesillos 18, 5748*)

Because he works from within, the *yetzer hara* knows
our weaknesses better than we do. He employs our bad character traits to lead us to sin. He convinces us that his advised
actions will result in physical pleasure, honor, or satisfaction. In reality, after the momentary pleasure of the sin has
subsided, we realize that we are left feeling empty and alien-
ated. The Torah warns us, "Neither yeast nor honey should
be brought as an offering to Hashem" (*Vayikra* 2:11). The
Kli Yakar says that yeast symbolizes pride, and honey symbolizes desire. They must both be avoided at all costs.

When a deed is engendered by pride or a desire for self-
indulgence, that is a clear warning that the *yetzer hara* is the
moving power behind it.

Rav Dovid of Lelov used to fast on weekdays. At the end of the week, he suddenly developed an over-powering thirst. Passing a gushing spring of water, he resolved to give up his fast and drink. He struggled to overcome his weakness, suppressed his thirst, and went on his way without even tasting the water.

After Rav Dovid had left the spring, he was suddenly possessed by a feeling of deep elation that he had managed to exercise such a measure of self-control. He immediately realized that this elation was not prompted by his better nature; on the contrary, it was his evil impulse that wished to inflate his ego with conceit for his self-control. In order to vanquish the feelings of pride, he retraced his steps, approached the spring, and drank from it.

(Sippurei Chassidim)

Food For Thought

The *yetzer hara* manipulates us, persuading us to…

- Pursue honor by achieving a position that will enable us to benefit the community.
- Take revenge against a friend to show him the truth.
- Avoid earnest service of Hashem out of "modesty."
- Associate with the wicked, befriending and flattering them, in order to bring them close.

The Power Of The *Yetzer Hara*

The *yetzer hara* is a powerful entity. Trying to overpower him is a constant battle, and the struggle of a lifetime (*Ohr Yahel, Noach*). Because the war against the *yetzer hara* is constant and unwavering, the *Mishnah* defines a strong person as one who *restrains* his inclination. He cannot be described as a person who has *restrained* his inclination, because as long as a person lives, he cannot declare that his evil inclination is vanquished. (*Ruach Chayim* 4:1) Even as a person overcomes his evil inclination, it grows stronger and attacks with increased vigor.

The war with the *yetzer hara* is without respite, for he is more powerful than the social and psychological forces he regularly employs. Even when the *yetzer tov* is victorious, the *yetzer hara* continues to let its voice be heard. Like a fly, he persistently returns, never leaving the person in peace. (*Mishlei Ha'Chofetz Chaim Ha'shalem*)

> *Rav Tovya, the Rav of Vilna, once visited the home of the Chofetz Chaim. A child playing in the house disturbed the Chofetz Chaim, so he suggested that she go play at the neighbors' home. A short time later, she returned and once again created a disturbance. The Chofetz Chaim asked her why she had come back so quickly. Why wasn't she playing with girls next door?*
>
> *"They weren't including me in their game," she answered. "I understood that I was not wanted."*
>
> *The Chofetz Chaim turned to the Rav and commented, "Look how a young child can tell when she is wanted and when she is not! If she is not welcome, she*

picks herself up and leaves. She is embarrassed to stay in a place where they are not happy to have her. All living things share that feeling of shame or fear—if they are chased away, they hesitate to return.

"The one exception is the fly. Even if you swat at it a thousand times, it immediately returns. Chase it from your face and it sits on your hand. Shake it from your hand and it settles on your ear. There is simply no getting rid of it, whether we are awake or whether we are trying to fall asleep.

"That is why the yetzer hara *is compared to the fly, for he never ceases to pester us. He has no fear and no shame. There is no way to get rid of him.* (Dugma Mi'sichos Avi 43) *A man must never rest in his battle with the* yetzer hara, *for even if you think that you are rid of him, he will soon return like a bothersome fly to try to tempt you."*

A victorious army, returning from war, marched triumphantly homeward. As they marched, the king noticed that his advisor looked worried, and he asked the advisor to tell him what was bothering him.

The advisor replied, "We have been victorious in this small skirmish, but now you stand before a major conflict, and I am very much concerned about the outcome."

"What are you talking about?" asked the king.

The advisor replied, "After this military victory, the true war begins—a war that never ends, the war against the evil inclination. For instance, will your present victory make you boastful?" He concluded, "In your joy over today's victory, do not fail to notice the traps that the evil inclination is setting out for you!"

(*Chovos Ha'levavos*)

When dealing with a conventional enemy, there is always hope a peace treaty will be signed one day, and the enmity will become a thing of the past. But our internal enemy is never ready for peace negotiations. The *yetzer hara* battles with a person from the moment of his birth, and he can never be pacified or defeated. He speaks to each person in his own language and takes advantage of every opportunity. The struggle lasts until the moment of death. Can there be a worse enemy than that? (*Midrash Tehillim* 34; *Me'sod Chachamim*, page 131)

A Rav who was a Kotzker chassid lay on his deathbed. His disciples, gathered around his bedside, observed that he appeared to be struggling. One of them bent down close to the Rav and asked if there was anything he could do. With his last ounce of strength, the Rav explained that his yetzer hara *was trying to persuade him to make a grand exit — to do something before he died that would have a tremendous impact on those present.*

(*Mi'prozdor Le'traklin*)

Some find that picturing the *yetzer hara* as a prosecutor, gloating over his victim, serves as an inspiration to find the strength to resist. Remember that after a person has fallen into his trap, the *yetzer hara* will stand at a distance, chuckling at the folly of his victim and enjoying his plight.

In *Gehinnom*, the soul that has sinned will see the *yetzer hara* standing before the Throne of Glory, saying mockingly, "What a fool you were! How pathetic. You didn't listen to Hashem—you chose to listen to me. Who am I anyway? I am just a lowly servant. Why did you trade an eternal world for a transient one?" (*Reishis Chochmah*)

> *The local prankster decided to play one of his famous practical jokes on the town fool. He planned to lure the fool to a swamp outside town and set him up as a laughingstock for all the townsfolk. He won the friendship of the fool with various treats and then invited him to accompany him for a walk. As night fell, the troublemaker whispered into the fool's ear, "I want to tell you an important secret, but first you must promise that you will not divulge it."*
>
> *The fool promised, and they shook hands on the deal.*
>
> *"Are you aware that there is a big swamp near here?"*
>
> *"I know," replied the fool. "I have also heard that it is deep and dangerous, and that anyone who wanders into it will sink, never to be seen again."*
>
> *"Stuff and nonsense!" exclaimed the prankster. "Do not believe such foolish talk. There is only a narrow strip of shallow swamp at the beginning of the field. Beyond it lays a vast treasure, buried by the*

losing armies after a great battle that was fought here long ago. Let's go into the swamp together, and we will split the treasure between us!"

The fool was convinced and excitedly rushed into the swamp, while the joker prudently stayed behind. The fool sank into the mud up to his waist. He struggled to get free, but only sank deeper with each desperate movement.

The fool saw the joker standing on safe, firm ground, and shouted to him, "Have pity on me! I am sinking. I am nearly up to my neck in mud! Hurry and save me. I don't care about the treasure any more. Just get me out of here!"

"What sweet talk," mocked the prankster. "You want me to pull you out of the swamp? I spent all that money on treats to persuade you to accompany me here. After all the time and bother it took to get you into the swamp, you want me to pull you out? I don't have the slightest intention of doing so. I am going to call all your friends to see you in this mess and to laugh at your foolishness. Only then will I have the pleasure of knowing that I have succeeded!"

The *yetzer hara* and *yetzer tov* must be equally enticing, like two magnets. One pulls us upwards, and the other downwards. We have equal access to both. (*Derech Hashem, Perek* 3)

Rabbi Shabsi Yudelevitz offers the following parable to explain this concept:

Suppose every person in the world started off with two pounds of yetzer hara and two pounds of yetzer tov. Exactly even. When the person does a mitzvah, his yetzer tov grows and flourishes. It is now, Baruch Hashem, two-and-a-quarter pounds. However because man must have an equal capacity to choose between good and evil, his yetzer hara must be given a booster of strength. Its power must also rise by a quarter of a pound so that free will can be maintained.

Of course the process is the same when a person sins. His yetzer tov grows thinner and his yetzer hara must be likewise diminished. Thus the integrity of his equal choice is maintained.

(Le'hagid, Bereishis)

Someone once complained to the Chofetz Chaim that his yetzer hara gave him no peace.

The Chofetz Chaim replied, "Do you see the clock over there? It is the source of much blessing. It religiously gives us the time of day so we can organize our day properly and get to shul on time.

"Now, consider how it works," the Chofetz Chaim continued. "To start it going, a person swings the pendulum to one side. The pendulum automatically swings back to the other side, and the constant back and forth keeps it ticking.

"So it is with us," he concluded. "The yetzer hara pulls us to one side, and the yetzer tov to the opposite

side. We fulfill our task in this world by resisting one and moving to the other."

(*Sichos Ha'Chofetz Chaim 23*)

The larger a clock, the greater the tension must be for the pendulum to keep swinging. This explains the concept of a greater person having a mightier *yetzer hara*. (*Succah 52a*) If he has a holier soul, then his *yetzer hara* must be commensurately stronger to maintain his free will.

A young Torah scholar with outstanding fear of G-d studied in the Kollel Kodshim established by the Chofetz Chaim. With the passage of time, his family grew and his children cried from hunger. Yet he learned with great diligence despite his penurious situation

He finally went to the Chofetz Chaim and explained that for lack of choice, he was entering the business world. He said, "I promise to set aside regular hours for Torah study. Since I know all too well how difficult it is to study when one is poverty-stricken, I will give a fifth of my earnings to support those who study Torah." He then asked that his rebbi *pray for his success.*

The Chofetz Chaim replied, "I will give you a piece of advice. If you want success, daven to He to Whom all wealth belongs (Niddah 70a). But remember that a promise to give charity is like a vow."

The man formally reiterated his commitment and received his rebbi's *blessing. He became so successful* in business that he was granted the right to settle in Moscow, a right granted to only a few privileged wealthy Jews.

The Chofetz Chaim was pleased to hear that his former student was keeping his original commitment to learn each day, but disappointed to discover that he was giving nothing to charity. When the Yeshivah's fundraisers told him that he was unapproachable, the Chofetz Chaim sighed.

Some time later, the Chofetz Chaim found himself in Moscow on yeshivah business. The city's prominent citizens came to greet him, including his former student.

When everyone who had come to pay their respects had left, the former student stayed behind. As soon as the two of them were alone, the man burst into tears.

The Chofetz Chaim asked, "What happened? Why are you crying? Is someone in the family ill?"

"Yes, Rebbi," he cried out in a choked voice, "I am the sick one, and I am stricken with a serious disease."

"What is your illness? Perhaps there is a remedy."

"There is a cure, Rebbi, but I am incapable of availing myself of it. I am afflicted with hardening of the heart and closure of the hand. I remember well my promise to give one fifth of my earnings to charity, but now my heart is like stone and my hand is sealed. I am like one paralyzed, and cannot part with a penny. I am totally dominated by the yetzer hara. Why has this happened to me?"

The Chofetz Chaim responded, "Calm down, and listen to my story.

"A villager came to the city before the holidays to buy food for Yom Tov. He asked the grocer to give him a ruble's worth of flour. The store's owner directed him to a bag behind him and told him to help himself.

"The villager took the bag, filled it up halfway, and put it on the scale. The grocer placed a weight on the other side to balance the scale and determine the price.

"'Anything else?' the grocer asked.

"'No,' the villager replied. But because there was still place in the sack, he took it back and filled it to the top. Then he returned it to the scale.

"After adding additional weights, the grocer told the villager, 'That will be five rubles.'

"The villager was surprised. 'But I asked you for one ruble's worth of flour,' he objected.

"The grocer replied, 'What did you think? That you could add more and more flour, and it wouldn't register? If you take out four-fifths of the flour, I will remove the equivalent weights, and you will only be required to pay one ruble.'

"Do you understand, my son?" the Chofetz Chaim gently asked. "To ensure man's free choice, Hashem always adjusts temptations as a person's circumstances change. A poor person is easily generous. Because he doesn't really have money to give, the yetzer hara leaves him alone. It was easy for you to make promises regarding your money before you had it.

However, the more 'flour' you placed on the scale, the more money you made — the more weights of miserliness were placed on the other side. The yetzer hara *grew along with your money. This is your test, and you must gather all your reserves and overpower this negative tendency."*

(*Mishlei Ha'Chofetz Chaim* 4)

FIGHTING THE *YETZER HARA*

Turning to Prayer

Rav Aharon Yosef Luria notes that there is only one proven method that will save us from the machinations of the *yetzer hara*: prayer (*Avodas Pnim*). Hashem comes to the assistance of those who turn to Him for help (*Yaaros Devash, Drush* 1).

It is proper to ask Hashem to save us from the *yetzer hara* (*Kiddushin* 81; *Chareidim*, Chapter 66). It should be the first step when faced with any challenge. In addition to regular daily *tefillos* to Hashem to save us from the *yetzer hara*, our Sages offer other prayers to be said when requesting Hashem's help against the *yetzer hara*. (See *Berachos* 16; *Berachos* 4; *Berachos* 60)

The *yetzer hara* was created so we will cry out to Hashem, "Save us!" Because the *yetzer hara* creates new challenges for us every day, we should begin each day with a request that Hashem help us avoid angering Him. He who cries out to Hashem to save him from the *yetzer hara* will not need to cry out to Hashem to save him from other things. (*Avodas Pnim*)

Food For Thought

Rav Shlomo David Yehoshua of Slonim explained that the verse, "Because she did not cry out in the city" (*Devarim* 22:24), is addressed to the man who did not cry out to Hashem to save him from the hands of the *yetzer hara*. When the *yetzer hara* tries to persuade us to sin, a Jew is held accountable if he does not appeal to Hashem for help.

(Va'yehi Ohr)

As soon as Havdalah ends, we should request that Hashem ensure that our coming week be free of sin. At the beginning of every month, and at the beginning of each year, the same request should be repeated. This is the meaning of the words of *Mishlei*, "Blessed is the person who is always afraid" (*Chareidim* 67).

If a person has a problem with a particular sin, he should pray that Hashem save him from that specific sin (*Yesod Ve'shoresh Ha'avodah*). When a person is in pain, he will naturally call out to Hashem, crying and pleading for compassion. At the very least, he should react the same way when he is tempted by sin, earnestly beseeching Hashem to save him from transgressing. (*SeferHa'chassidim* 28) He should pray with the intensity of a person praying for his only child who is dying, for sin is the greatest imaginable agony that a person can endure (*Peleh Yoetz, Aveirah*). Suffering in this world is limited, but suffering in the Next World has no limit (*Sefer Ha'chassidim* 28).

Always On Guard

Those who imagine they have gained the upper hand in their battle with the *yetzer hara* are harboring a dangerous illusion. We must remain on our guard at all times.

> *Rav Yitzchok of Vorki once woke up in middle of the night and felt an overpowering impulse to take a pinch of snuff. He stretched out his hand to reach for the box, which was just a little too far away for him to grasp, and then reconsidered. Should he get up from his bed to get the box? If he did, he would be acceding to his desires, and he would find himself more easily persuaded on a different occasion. But if he did not get up, he might be yielding to the selfish impulse of laziness. If he allowed such sloth to become a habit, it might cause him to neglect his religious duties in the future. He finally reached the perfect solution: he got out of bed to deny any hint of laziness, but he did not yield to the impulsive desire to take a pinch of snuff!*
>
> (*Yalkut Sippurim*)

A person should employ any tactics at his disposal to control the *yetzer hara*. When the wife of Potifar tried to ensnare Yosef, the Torah tells us that he left his garments in her hand and fled (*Bereishis* 39:12). The commentaries question why he risked leaving his garments behind, knowing that she would use them to incriminate him. They explain that Yosef did not pause long enough to retain his garment because he feared that if he didn't flee immediately, the wife of Potifar might induce him to sin.

When the Ponovezher Rav had to deal with women who attempted to shake hands, he would take off his hat and hold it with both hands while he bowed in greeting.

When a woman sat down next to Rav Shlomo Zalmen Auerbach on the bus, he rose from his seat, pulled the cord to alert the bus driver to stop for him, and got off the bus. It did not matter to him that he had to walk some kilometers to reach his destination.

EXERCISE

Having trouble getting up in the morning? Get a flying alarm clock. Once you retrieve it, it will be hard to return to your bed. Having trouble staying awake while learning on the couch? Find another place to study that is less comfortable.

The *Gemara* quotes ShimonHa'tzaddik:

It happened once that a *nazir* from the south came [to the BeisHa'mikdash to bring his offering]. He had beautiful eyes, a pleasing complexion, and rows of wavy locks. I said to him, "My son, what has impelled you to destroy your beautiful hair?" [At the conclusion of the period of *nezirus*, the *nazir* must have all his hair shorn.]

He replied, "I was a shepherd for my father in my city. It happened once that I went to a spring to fill my pail and I took note of my reflection [in the water]. I felt my evil inclination rush on me — it sought to drive me from this world! I said to it, 'Wicked one! Why do you take pride in a world that is not your own, in one who will in the end be worms and maggots? I swear that I will [become a *nazir* and] have you [his hair] shorn for the sake of Heaven.'"

I [ShimonHa'tzaddik] immediately arose and kissed him on his head. I told him, "May there be many more *nezirim* like you in Israel! It is regarding you that the Torah writes, "When a man or woman will express themselves to vow the vow of a *nazir*, to consecrate themselves to Hashem" (*Nedarim* 9b).

Rashi comments that when the young man observed his own handsomeness, he felt himself being overcome by an urge to sin. He perceived that becoming enamored of his own good looks was the work of his *yetzer hara*. He saw the wicked person he might become. He peered into the future and feared what the future could bring. He addressed the *yetzer hara* instructing him to look for other youths to lead astray. His subsequent reaction illustrates a valuable tool of confronting the *yetzer hara*. The young man refused to permit the *yetzer hara* to draw him after the vanities of this world. Instead, he decided to become a *nazir* and shave off his beautiful locks for the sake of Hashem, thus subduing the *yetzer hara* urging him to sin. (*Inspiration and Insight, Parshas Naso*) Because he was strong enough not to fall into the *yetzer hara*'s trap he deserved a kiss from Shimon Ha'tzaddik.

> When Rav Yehudah Leib Chasman taught this Gemara, *he would cry out the words of the* nazir *to his* yetzer hara, "Wicked one, why do you take pride in a world that is not your own?" To his listeners, he

seemed to be rebuking them for their attachment to
the vanities of this world.

(Tenuas Ha'mussar)

The *Gemara* offers another example of using desperate measures for desperate occasions.

When he was faced with a difficult test, Rav Am-
ram feared that he would soon be overpowered by
his yetzer hara. *He called out at the top of his lungs,*
"There is a fire in the house of Amram! There is a fire
in the house of Amram!" Everyone gathered to help
Amram put out the fire, and thus Amram was pre-
vented from sinning. He used the power of embar-
rassment to overcome his evil inclination.

(Kiddushim 81a)

In more recent times, a Torah scholar invented a truly imaginative solution to overcoming the *yetzer hara*.

A Torah scholar living in Yerushalayim support-
ed his family by distributing milk throughout the
religious community in the early hours of the morn-
ing. Everywhere he went, he left an unpleasant odor
in his wake. No one could figure out what caused
the terrible smell, until someone asked the scholar
directly. He explained that because the milk distri-
bution brought him in contact with the women in
the community, he was afraid that the yetzer hara

might lead him into forbidden interaction with his customers. Therefore, before leaving his house each morning, he poured vinegar on his head. The strong, unpleasant aroma ensured that no one would get too close.

(*Aleinu Le'shabeiach*, page 550)

● ●

EXERCISE

Try talking to your *yetzer hara*. It's a marvelous tool. If he manages to disturb your devotion during prayer, say to him, "You succeeded in distracting me, but now I will silently repeat the paragraph with devotion."

If the *yetzer hara* has succeeded in preventing you from doing a certain important task, instruct him, "For the next five minutes I am doing something important. Do not get involved."

At the end of the day, when he tries to persuade you that you are not fit to do a mitzvah because you are so tired, say to him, "Keep quiet! You had me in your clutches all day. Did it ever occur to you that the *yetzer tov* is occasionally allowed to win?"

● ●

The altruistic individual who is preoccupied with the needs of others is accustomed to relegating his own needs to second place. He acquires a lot of experience in subduing his egotistical drives. This makes love of a fellow Jew an excellent preparatory tool in subduing the *yetzer hara*. (Rabbi Avrohom Erlanger)

Learning Torah

Chazal instruct us that the best way to counter the *yetzer hara* is with the Torah (*Kiddushin* 30b). The *Mesilas Yesharim* adds that no one knows the *yetzer hara*'s strengths like Hashem Who created it, and the only way to conquer it is with Torah! The wicked person is reviled for not having studied Torah, for if he had studied, he would not have remained a wicked person. (Rav Sholom Schwadron, quoting Rav Yehudah Leib Chasman in *Lev Shalom, Bereishis*, page 52)

The study of *mussar*, which deals with the seriousness of sin, enables us to take a proper inventory and weigh the losses incurred by a sin against the momentary pleasures it offers us. (*Bava Basra* 78b). Sometimes, learning the halachos relating to our particular challenges can help us overcome the *yetzer hara*.

When a pharmacist mixes together the ingredients of a medication, he carefully adds the precise dose of each required drug. Would an unlearned layman attempt to mix the ingredients himself, choosing items from the shelves at random? Only a trained expert can be trusted to prepare the correct mixture.

It is the same when it comes to dealing with our *yetzer hara*. Alone, we do not have the knowledge to defeat him. Only with the help of Hashem's Torah can we hope to be successful. (*Nefesh Ha'Chaim*, Gate 4, Chapter 32)

> *There were two armies engaged in an ongoing battle. One day, one side would win; the next day, the other would prevail. Their numbers dwindled as many were killed in action, but neither side managed to destroy their enemy.*

Then one of the generals carried out a bold plan. With ten warriors at his side, he crept into the enemy camp under cover of darkness. They readily overcame the armory guards and stole all the weapons and ammunition that were stored there. Then they silently returned to their own camp.

The next day, their battalions attacked. The enemy ran to replenish their ammunition, only to discover that the armory was empty! With no way to defend themselves, they were forced to surrender and were taken prisoner.

The *yetzer hara* is our enemy, whom we have fought for many generations. Sometimes, we win; sometimes, he defeats us. When this wicked tempter sees that he cannot win the war, he decides to use a devious strategy and purloin our ammunition. He knows that our ammunition is the Torah, and that without Torah we can never hope to overcome him. The *yetzer hara* therefore invests a lot of effort into distracting us from the study of our holy Torah, thus robbing us of our main weapon.

We must strengthen ourselves in the study of Torah so we can overcome our *yetzer hara*. The Torah is our best and only weapon and armor in the battle with the *yetzer hara*. (*Shemiras Ha'lashon, Shaar Ha'Torah*, Chapter 8)

INSPIRATION

The Kotzker Rebbe sought chassidim who would not be tempted by their *yetzer hara* — not because they refused to listen to his advice, but because they had no time to listen to his chatter.

(*Rosh Golas Ariel*)

"When a person is occupied with Torah and good deeds, he is able to control his *yetzer hara*" (*Avodah Zarah* 5:2).

Rabbi Ben Zion Abba Shaul observed that rainwater flowing from the mountaintop into a dry wadi will go to waste. The wise man digs ditches that guide the downpour to water his field. In the same way, we can utilize our natural propensities in a constructive manner. Emotions should be expressed through superior traits, such as generosity, courage, love of Hashem's servants, and hatred of His enemies. "Only Torah, not the study of psychology or sociology, can help us refine our inner selves and achieve clarity in our lives" (*Hamaspik Le'ovdei Hashem*; *Ohr Le'tziyon*).

Nefesh Ha'Chaim explains that each specific temptation has a portion of the Torah to serve as its antidote. A person should identify his weaknesses and find the Torah texts that address them. Each manifestation of the *yetzer hara* can be countered by Aggadic teachings of our Sages that address that particular inclination. (*From a Pure Fire*, page 74)

Without Substance

"There was a small town [the body] with only a few inhabitants [the limbs]. A mighty king [the *yetzer hara*] surrounded it and built great siege works over it [guiding it to do evil]. Present was a poor, wise man [the *yetzer tov*], who by his wisdom saved the town. Yet no one remembers that poor man [when the *yetzer hara* gains dominion, no one remembers the *yetzer tov*]." (*Koheles* 9:14–15; *Nedarim* 32)

Rav Sholom Schwadron raises several questions relating to the *Gemara's* interpretation of these verses in *Koheles*:

Why did a mighty king need to wage war against a small town, and why did the king require a great siege? Couldn't a small contingent have taken over the village?

Once the mighty king arrived with his siege equipment, why didn't he invade the city and conquer it? Why did he merely surround the city and construct siege works, without taking further steps to conquer the city?

The city's savior appears to be a rather feeble specimen who opts to save its citizens using only his wisdom. How does wisdom prevail over missiles?

Last, how is it that the savior is forgotten when the next siege begins and the same scenario repeats itself all over again? Why don't the people of the city remember the wisdom that saved them the first time?

Rav Sholom found a resolution to all these questions when he visited the wax museum in London. He watched from a distance as visitors respectfully approached the two armed guards who stood at the entrance to the museum. The visitors would politely ask for directions or instructions, but neither sentry offered a reply.

There was a good reason for this, of course: the two guards were actually carved from wax! Rav Sholom saw how the visitors took a second look at the sentries, and how they would ultimately smile and laugh when they realized that the guards were actually simulated fakes.

Rav Sholom now had the answers to all his questions. The siege works of the mighty king were all forged from wax, and the king himself was no more than a wax figure. That is why he needed such frightful-looking siege works. The besieged townspeople would imagine the terrors that lurked beyond the siege weapons, and the fear and confusion would cause such panic that they didn't dare refuse to yield to him. But in reality, all their fears were based on a fantasy.

The wise man required no weapons, for there was nothing to fight at all. The secret of his strength was the revelation of the deception, so all can see that the *yetzer hara*'s bark is far worse than his bite. There was no need to panic, because the king's arsenal was only a mirage. He himself is an illusion, and his soldiers and weapons have no substance.

But despite a person's accomplishments, the *yetzer hara* never retreats completely. Man is liable to forget the wisdom he has acquired. A person must remember his previous victories and make sure that it doesn't happen again.

One niggling question remains: How did the wise man discover that the mighty king was a mirage? The answer is simple. He did not have to be a prophet or a miracle worker; he only had to think and observe. He asked the same questions that Rav Sholom posed. Why the huge siege? Why not an actual attack? The questions and observations let to valuable conclusions and the triumph of the town.

We must learn from the wise man to cling to our commitment to Hashem. Even if it is initially difficult, our ultimate victory will be pleasant and sweet, and the initial difficulties will be forgotten.

Rav Shwadron offers a parable from daily life. Reuven dislikes Shimon. One day Reuven bumps into Levi, who has to do business with Shimon and asks Reuven for advice. Here is a rare opportunity for Reuven to hurt Shimon financially. Deep in his heart, a raging confrontation swirls. Let us listen to the argument that takes place....

The yetzer tov *points out that Reuven is biased, and saying anything negative is forbidden.*

The yetzer hara *has a long list of reasons and justifications for speaking. Certainly, Shimon is not included among those of those of whom it is forbidden to speak evil. No doubt it is a mitzvah to publicize his wickedness! Anyway, Reuven is required by Torah law to protect Levi against potential damage, and there is every reason to suspect that Shimon will misbehave in the future, just as he has misbehaved in the past.... On and on, the* yetzer hara *enumerates numerous reasons for burying Shimon forever.*

At that point, Reuven should stop and ask himself: if it is permitted to speak, why the need for such a long list of justifications? The truth is streamlined and direct, and requires no elaborate edifice. The list is so long because it must prop up falsehood!

Rav Sholom concludes with an incident from his own life that illustrates the powers of the *yetzer hara* to construct arguments of delusion.

When Rav Sholom was still a boy studying in ye-shivah, he and his friend decided to stop eating Tnuva products because the company was open on Shabbos.

In those days, the standard of living in Yerusha-layim was quite low. Necessities were hard to come by, and luxuries were nonexistent. His supper each night consisted of a single slice of bread and a cup of black coffee. Additions to this meager meal were few and far between.

The same night that Rav Sholom and his friend agreed to stop consuming Tnuva products, he ar-rived home to find that his mother had set out a Tnu-va leben *with his meal. Rav Sholom had no father, and his mother worked very hard to support the fam-ily. This additional treat must have been purchased with great difficulty.*

Rav Sholom remembered the day's resolution and determined not to eat the leben, *but the* yetzer hara *does not sleep.*

As Rav Sholom writes, the arguments began. "First, the yetzer hara *challenged me, 'What about the commandment not to waste food?'*

"I considered whether this was reason to eat the leben. *My* yetzer tov *reminded me of my resolve. I put the spoon down.*

"The yetzer hara *was not finished. 'What about the obligation to honor your mother? How will she feel if you reject the food she gives you?' The* yetzer tov *re-minded me that I had decided not to eat Tnuva prod-ucts for a good reason.*

"*The* yetzer hara *tried again. He reminded me that my mother was a widow, and that it is forbidden to cause a widow anguish. I took the spoon into my hand again.*

"*The* yetzer tov *whispered into my ear, 'Remember your decision.' I lowered the spoon.*

"*The* yetzer hara *went on and on, without stopping. I got up, took the* leben, *and put it back into the cabinet.*

"*In the morning, when my mother saw that I hadn't eaten the* leben, *she commented, 'Shloimka, I see you didn't feel like eating the* leben.*' No complaints, no anger, no anguish. All the* yetzer hara's *illusionary arguments were just that—fantasies!*

"*When I shared my experiences with my friend, he had the same story to tell me. His mother, too, had prepared* leben *for him....*"

(*Lev Shalom, Bereishis*, pages 54–60)

In reality, the *yetzer hara* has no substance. Sadly, most people are too quick to raise a white flag of surrender. The wise individual, recognizing the *yetzer hara*'s irrelevance, reacts more aggressively.

The *yetzer hara* is like a prankster running through a crowd, showing his tightly closed fist. No one knows what it is he is holding. He goes up to each person and asks, "What do you suppose I have in my hand?" Each person imagines that the closed hand contains just what he desires most, and hurries to run after the prankster. Then, when he has tricked them all into following him, he opens his hand to reveal what it contains. It is completely empty!

The same is true of the *yetzer hara*. The *yetzer hara* promises happiness in the future. As a rule he does not keep his promises. His checks are written in disappearing ink. He tricks the world, fooling people into following him. Rebbe Nachman called the *yetzer hara* the *koach ha'midameh*, the power of illusion. Everyone thinks that his hand contains what he needs. But in the end, the *yetzer hara* opens his hand, and there is nothing there to fulfill any desire. Worldly pleasures are just like sunbeams in a dark room: they may actually seem solid, but when a person tries to grasp a sunbeam, he finds nothing in his hand. (*Reb Nachman's Wisdom* #6)

Food For Thought

A terrifying bandit sat at the crossroads, threatening all passersby. One wise traveler observed that the bandit was actually aged and decrepit, so when he demanded that he hand over his valuables, the traveler attacked him instead.

(*Midrash Rabbah, Bereishis* 22:12)

Our Friend, The *Yetzer Hara*

The *yetzer hara* attempts to prevent a person from doing good. This service is vital, for he provides us with the opportunity to exercise free will, choosing good and life in the face of temptation and immorality. Without temptation, the choice of good would be self-evident. The *yetzer hara* does battle with our emotions — not because he desires that we succumb, but rather so that we might strengthen our commitment to Torah by overcoming the challenges we face.

Yaakov Avinu encountered the *yetzer hara* in a face-to-face struggle. They wrestled all night, and the *yetzer hara* surely used his most powerful arsenal of seduction, temptation, and desire. Towards daybreak, the *yetzer hara* was forced to admit defeat — Yaakov had the better of him.

"Now you must let me go," the *yetzer hara* declared. "Day is breaking and my time has come to sing *shirah* before Hashem!"

"First bless me," Yaakov said.

"You don't understand," the angel objected. "In all my years of existence, from the day Hashem created me until now, I have never once had the opportunity to sing *shirah*. Now, finally, my time has come. Please let me go and offer songs of praise before my Creator!" (*Chullin* 91b)

The angel's excuse seems somewhat suspect. The *yetzer hara* had existed since Creation, yet his only opportunity to sing *shirah* just happened to coincide with his defeat at Yaakov's hands? Is this merely surprising coincidence, or something more?

In reality, it was the *yetzer hara*'s defeat that granted him the opportunity to sing *shirah*. After an all-night battle, Yaakov demonstrated that he had complete and total control over his emotions and desires. He took hold of the *yetzer hara* — now Yaakov was in command.

"Set me free," said the *yetzer hara*, "for this is a time of great joy for me, and I must go and sing praises to Hashem. My mission has been accomplished. It is now time to offer my song before the Creator: I have encountered the man who has triumphed over me!" (Rav Yisroel of Koznitz)

INSPIRATION

If you find yourself in the throes of temptation, try reminding yourself that the *yetzer hara* actually *wants* you to reject his overtures. Remember that the same *yetzer hara* who gives you perverse feelings and desires wants you to overcome temptation! Picture the *yetzer hara* watching you and cheering you on, and you can make use of the opportunity to exercise free will and choose good. Conversely, imagine if you succumb to your desires and sin. "You fool!" the *yetzer hara* exclaims. "How could you? You missed the point completely! I never actually intended that you should sin — I was just trying to give you an opportunity for spiritual growth and self-perfection!"

(Beis Yitzchok)

Shemiras Ha'lashon

The Gift Of Speech

The gift of speech is man's crowning characteristic. That small bit of air exiting from our mouths may seem to have little import — but, in fact, it is speech that distinguishes man from beast. Value your exalted status; do not allow your tongue to bring you down to the level of an animal. (*Binah Le'ittim, Derush 3*)

A surgeon consulted Rav Shach for help in resolving a tragic dilemma. A patient had a growth in his neck. To get rid of the tumor, the surgeon had the option of removing the larynx or the esophagus. The former would deprive the patient of his speech, while the latter would significantly affect his ability to eat.

Rav Shach advised that the larynx should not be touched. Retaining man's speech is more vital than the smooth functioning of his digestive system, for this ability is what elevates man above animals.

("*Mi Yirpeh Lach*" from a lecture
by Rav Yitzchok Silberstein)

Food For Thought

Rabbi Chisdah said that anyone who speaks *lashon hara* should be stoned (*Archin* 16). Why? Because he has taken the gift that elevates him above animals and defiled it. Being pelted with a stone suggests that he would have been better off without the ability to speak—mute as a stone.

(*Einei Yitzchok*)

The soul's aspiration are given physical form and come into the world through speech (*Targum Onkelos, Bereishis* 2:7). Although one might assume that intellect is the essence of mankind, it is through speech that human intellect is expounded and disseminated. Without speech, our thoughts cannot become concrete. That is probably the reason that man is defined as a *medaber*, a speaker.

Until Helen Keller mastered sign language, her life was limited to direct experiences, such as the sun on her face and rain on her hand. Only when she grasped the power of language was she able to experience feelings.

INSPIRATION

Rabbi Zalman Sorotzkin writes, "Through speech and writing, man's practical and theoretical innovations in all realms of knowledge are transmitted to others, and likewise, each generation passes on the knowledge it inherited from its predecessors, as well as its own additions. In the course of many generations, man has succeeded in working over and refining the new material revealed by Hashem, achieving an extraordinary level of science and technology. Without speech and writing, the transfer of knowledge between contemporaries would be impossible and man's intellect would stagnate and degenerate."

(Oznaim Le'Torah, Bereishis 2:7)

Using Speech Correctly

Speech should be used to serve Hashem *(Alshich Shemos* 28:31)

> *Rav Elya Lopian would occasionally resort to using sharp humor to make certain points that he felt were best communicated through that medium. His audience would shake with laughter at his witticisms. Rav Lopian, however, would remain serious even at these times. It was clear that he was completely in control of his tongue and did not allow himself to be carried away with what he was saying. Each phrase and comment was carefully measured.*

"Who is the man who desires life?" *(Tehillim* 34:13). The quality of guarding one's tongue makes one deserving of being called a man.

Food For Thought

A house full of holy texts is not exempt from a mezuzah on its door. This makes the mezuzah a tangible reminder to the very righteous of the importance of sanctifying one's mouth — the entrance to one's self.

(*Chasam Sofer on Torah, Korach*)

Rav Yehudah son of Shushan appeared to the chassid Rav Lapidos in a dream. His face shone like the sun, and each hair on his beard glowed like a torch. When he was asked what he did to deserve such brilliant light, he explained that he had never spoken unnecessarily.

(*Reishis Chochmah, Shaaar Ha'ahavah, Chapter 6*)

Rav Avrohom Horowitz guarded his tongue successfully. When he passed away, his family inscribed three words on his tombstone: "Shomer Piv U'leshono — He guarded his mouth and his tongue," followed by the details of his birth and death.

His son-in-law, Reb Nochum Dovid Herman, asked Rav Avrohom's father how Rav Avrohom had managed to guard his tongue so well.

The father related, "When he became bar mitzvah he was called up for maftir *and said the* beracha, *'Who gave us the Torah of truth and planted a life of eternity in our midst.' As he walked back to his seat I heard him say, 'Ribono shel Olam, I saw in the* mussar seforim *how terrible* lashon hara *is. I accept upon myself to never to speak* lashon hara *for the rest of my life!' And that is what he did.*"

(*From a Pure Fire*, pages 36–37)

INSPIRATION

Although the *Mishnah* states, "I have seen nothing better for the body than silence" (*Avos* 3:13), only in regard to corporeal things is silence golden (*Sefas Emes*). An uncommunicative individual can be faulted for not making use of his greatest asset, the faculty of speech that lends substance to his intellectual powers. The ideal course is paved with speech. Talk about constructive topics, which is of use in our relationship with Hashem and others. According to Rav Yechezkel Sarna, such was the habit of the Chofetz Chaim, who never sat silently while in the company of others.

(*Marbitzei Torah U'mussar*)

The mouth is an important vessel in our service of Hashem. How is a vessel defined? A vessel changes the status of an item. A pot converts raw food to cooked food. A broom upgrades a dirty floor to a clean floor. A sewing machine transforms material into finished clothing.

In what way is the mouth a vessel? When we designate an animal as a sacrifice, it becomes holy to Hashem. (*Chayei Olam*, Chapter 49) By saying *Kiddush*, we change the status of a regular cup of wine to holy Shabbos wine. With the blessing *"al netilas lulav,"* we change a palm frond into an elevated entity in the service of Hashem. Our words have an impact on the higher spiritual worlds, constructing and destroying spiritual edifices.

When the mouth is kept untainted through the observance of *shemiras ha'lashon*, it is equal in holiness to the vessels in the *Beis Ha'mikdash*. It is worth the great effort to keep it pure!

> *When Rav Yisrael Abuchatzeira was ten years old, he encountered a group of children who were fighting, and he censured the child who started the fight. Later that day, he recounted the incident to his father. "I was so angry at those children," he told him, "that I nearly cursed the instigator." His father, Rav Mas'ud, listened carefully to Rav Yisrael's story, and used it as a springboard to teach him a lesson that eventually became the cornerstone of Rav Yisrael's way of life. "My son, you are destined for greatness, and one day, all that escapes your lips will be fulfilled. As a result, you must only bless and speak well of others, and never curse anyone."*
>
> *(Yated Ne'eman)*

> *Rav Shlomo Zalman Dalinsky was very careful with his speech. One day he was helping out in his wife's store when a youngster known for his vulgar language entered to buy something. The salesman asked him to leave, and the teenager responded with*

a string of juicy curses. Rav Zalman asked the boy to come in, cordially served him, and then asked if he could now repeat those curses in the form of blessings. Thus he taught the lad how to express himself in a positive manner.

(*Tenuas Ha'mussar*)

A man was drafted into the Russian army right after the birth of his firstborn son. His wife was overwhelmed by the evil tidings, for this induction was often the equivalent of a death warrant. Rav Yosef Levenstein, the city's Rav, promised that the father would be back for the pidyon ha'ben.

The man was in the midst of a court-martial before an anti-Semitic military court for a minor infraction. His life hung in the balance. While intently focused on begging Hashem to spare him, it suddenly occurred to our hero to pretend that he was lame. He began to walk as if one leg was shorter than the other.

The judge made fun of his gait. The courtroom was overcome with laughter, and the case was dismissed. The man was sent home and arrived right in time for his son's pidyon ha'ben.

Those present wanted to know if the Rav's prediction was a result of ruach ha'kodesh.

"No!" the Rav emphatically replied. "But I am always very careful with my speech. I avoid saying anything inappropriate, so my words are respected and fulfilled."

(*Sipurim Yerushalmiyim*)

Effortless Speech

Speech is a faculty that requires the least advance preparation. While a thought process must precede a deed, man says the most complicated words effortlessly.

Speech is so facile because man is required to master the Torah; if too much effort is required to convert thoughts into words, it would take much longer to achieve mastery in Torah study. We are also meant to use our speech in beneficial ways, such as by encouraging and helping others. This is why we were given the ability to easily utter numerous words in a short period of time.

> *A person can readily utter about two hundred words a minute. To prove this, a Rav once had his student repeat the nearly fifty words of the prayer, "These are the things that have no limit," four times in succession. It took him exactly one minute.*
>
> (*Pnei Mayer, page 47*)

Unfortunately, when it comes to *lashon hara* and other negative speech, this gift becomes a drawback. If we had to think before speaking, we would keep our destructive conversations in check, thus saving ourselves countless sins. Hashem is anguished when He sees His precious bequest used for such unworthy goals. How tragic when this valuable gift becomes a tool of destruction! (*Toras Ha'bayis*, Chapter 2)

> *The king's new palace needed drapes and upholstery, and members of the court required new royal garments. Soon the country's most renowned weaver*

was standing before the king. He was supplied with a great warehouse of cotton and wool and hundreds of weaving machines. The king's designers were on hand to give the weaver a description of what the king desired.

The finance minister gave the weaver a tour of the machinery he would be using. After they had inspected all of them, the weaver turned to a strange new machine with wires running from its side. "And what is this for?" he asked.

"This machine is powered by electricity," the minister explained. "It can weave in minutes what the other machines do in a day. But you must be extremely careful. For if the slightest thing goes wrong, this machine can ruin more material in minutes than all the others can produce in a day."

(*Chofetz Chaim*)

Food For Thought

"Be not rash with your mouth, and let not your heart be hasty to utter a word before Hashem; for Hashem is in heaven and you are on earth, so let your words be few. For a dream comes from concern, and foolish talk from many words."

(*Koheles* 5:1)

Our mouths are more powerful than we realize. "Death and life are in the power of the tongue" (*Mishlei* 18:21). The *malach ha'maves* revealed that he is nourished by *lashon* hara (*Pri Tzaddik, Parshas Korach*). By speaking *lashon hara*, one brings death to himself. When one speaks words of Torah, on the other hand, he grants himself life.

A man was rushed to the hospital for emergency surgery. At the post-op visit, the surgeon discovered another medical problem that could not be ignored. The man was distressed to hear that he needed more surgery — but that was nothing compared to how he felt a few weeks later, when he had finally recovered from his ordeal. He was stricken by another medical condition, necessitating yet another surgical procedure. There appeared to be no end in sight.

A relative who was a Gerrer chassid suggested that the man's son go to the Gerrer Rebbe, the Pnei Menachem, for a blessing.

When the son told the Rebbe about the strange series of surgeries his father required, the Rebbe said, "Tell me a little about your family's behavior at the Shabbos table."

A look of embarrassment suffused the young man's features. "Our Shabbos table is quite pathetic," he admitted.

The Rebbe pressed him for details. "In what way? Do you discuss other people at your Shabbos table?"

The son nodded unhappily.

The Rebbe bore down on him. "Do you perhaps tear people to pieces at your Shabbos table?"

"At our Shabbos table we dissect one person after another," the son confessed.

"There is your answer," replied the Rebbe. "This is why your father is being dissected so often. If you stop dismembering others and switch to discussing words of Torah at your Shabbos table, the need for surgeries will stop."

When the son informed his father of the Rebbe's recommendation, the man undertook to give his Shabbos table a facelift. The need for surgical procedures became a distant memory.

(*Borchi Nafshi, Shemos*, pages 187–188)

Food For Thought

When Yaakov said the words, "With whomever they are found [Lavan's *terafim*] shall not live," he never dreamed that this would result in the premature death of his beloved wife.

(*Dugmah Me'sichos Avi*)

After 120 years, each person will be shown all the repercussions of his speech, including the worlds he sustained and the worlds he destroyed (*Chagigah* 5; *Toras Ha'bayis*; *Derashas Rav Chaim Volozhiner*). Words that have been uttered have a life of their own. Let us hope that they will never stand up against us.

The Chida wrote seventy-one seforim, sixty-eight of which were printed—the numerical equivalent of his name, Chaim. There is one common denominator to the three unprinted seforim: *the title's reference to concealment. The first was called* The Hidden Light; *the second,* Internal Rooms; *and the third,* Unseen Words. *The titles he chose ultimately determined their fate, and they remained hidden, internal, and unseen.*

(*Aleinu Le'shabeiach,* pages 94–95)

Rav Meir Simchah of Dvinsk was unable to attend the funeral of the Kovna Rav, Rav Yitzchok Elchanan Spector. Rav Meir Simchah asked a close relative who attended the funeral if a certain prominent maggid *had delivered a eulogy.*

The relative replied that because there was such a huge crowd it was decided that this well-known speaker should address the crowd gathered outside. A makeshift podium was set up with a table and chair hoisted on top. But before he could begin speaking, the podium shifted and the speaker fell, hurting his head. In the end, someone else spoke in his stead.

"I thought as much," said Rav Meir Simchah. "I knew he wouldn't be able to eulogize the Rav."

"How did you know?" asked his relative.

"Seventeen years ago, that maggid *mentioned to me that he had a din Torah with someone before Rav Yitzchok Elchonon. The Kovna Rav had declared him guilty, and the* maggid *was so angered by his loss that he declared that the Kovna Rav was biased.*

"I remember telling him that he would not be given the opportunity to eulogize the Kovna Rav because of what he said. I was certain that he would be denied the chance to speak."

(Sheal Avicha Ve'yagedcha, Vol. II)

INSPIRATION

The Rambam points out that there are five types of speech.

The first is speaking words that are a mitzvah, such as Torah and prayer.

The second is forbidden speech, which includes cursing, profanities, falsehood, *lashon hara*, and *rechilus*.

Tasteless words are the third category, and refer to idle talk and speaking disparagingly of ethical behavior.

The next is worthwhile speech, which is the praise of virtuous behavior and the degrading of negative conduct.

The final category, permissible speech, revolves around such things as business, food, and budget.

The Imrei Emes was once traveling by horse and carriage. The driver asked one of his fellow passengers a question, to which he replied, "Tak, tak." The Rebbe asked for the meaning of the words, and was told that it means, "Yes, yes."

The Rebbe expressed his wonder that the driver saw the need to repeat the word. Wasn't once enough?

(Rosh Golas Ariel, page 446)

Talk of a secular nature can be a great time waster. Unnecessary chitchat can be addictive. Such speech can all too easily slip into unpleasant, negative, or forbidden speech.

While the Imrei Emes was conversing with his Rebbetzin she mentioned a certain chassid who had a swarthy complexion, whom she identified as "Mottel, the dark fellow."

"One doesn't say such a thing about a fellow Jew," commented the Rebbe.

"So what should one say?" she asked.

"Mottel, the tall fellow," he replied....

During the Rebbe's first visit to Eretz Yisroel, a chassid complained to him that the head of his kollel was withholding his stipend.

When the Rebbe raised the question with this functionary, he reacted by saying, "That man's a fool."

The Rebbe cut him short. "Is that how one speaks about a Jew?" he protested.

A chassid asked whether he should visit wealthy relatives in America who had promised they would help him marry off his son. The Rebbe stated his opinion that for such a purpose, it would be worthwhile to undertake the trip.

The chassid then mentioned that he had once visited America and did not like the look of the Jews there.

Before he managed to say another word, the Rebbe interrupted. "Is this the place to speak lashon hara*?"*

(Rebbes of Ger)

The Maggid of Vilkomir points out that we were endowed with two barriers for the tongue — our teeth and lips — to remind us that we must think before we speak and consider whether what we are about to say is worth saying (*Einei Yitzchok*).

Food For Thought

Friendly conversations should focus on matters of interest, not people of interest. There are homes where members of the family are careful never to discuss others.

(*Igeres Le'horim*)

The Chofetz Chaim notes that before speaking, one should cautiously measure his words, make sure that they are accurate, and ensure that every word that is said complies with halachah.

> *Our Sages advise that a person should adopt silence as a profession. "What is a person's skill in this world? To act as though mute" (Chullin 89a). In a lecture at the yeshivah in Kelm, the Chofetz Chaim clarified the profession of silence by citing the following analogy:*
>
> *A man worked hard to earn a living. One day he was delighted to discover that he had come into a large inheritance. Suddenly he was wealthy!*

"Until now, you had to work hard to earn a living," an astute friend remarked. *"From now on, though, you will have a different concern — you will focus on not losing your wealth in an unsound venture."*

If only we were wise enough to protect our mitzvah investments, and not lose them with ill-advised words!

(*Mayim Chayim, Shemos*)

● ●

EXERCISE

Imagine that your conversations are being recorded. Imagine how embarrassing it would be to have someone play back your conversations in public.

● ●

When the Jewish People returned to Eretz Yisroel after the Babylonian exile, it was discovered that the book with the records of each family's lineage had been lost. How did people determine who belonged to a family that was of pure Jewish lineage? Candidates who had mastered the art of silence were the first choice. (*Kiddushin* 71b)

Food For Thought

Silence is good for the wise; how much more so for the foolish.

(*Pesachim* 99a)

A word is worth a *sela*, but silence is worth two.

(*Megillah* 18a)

Silence is a fence around wisdom.

(*Avos* 3: 13)

When I speak, I have reason to regret. But when I am silent, I have nothing to regret. Before I speak, I am master over my words. Once the words leave my mouth, they rule over me.

(*Mimayanos Ha'netzach*)

When Rav Shlomo Wolbe eulogized Rav Kluft, he told the following story:

Rav Kluft's first rabbanus *position in Eretz Yisroel was in Rechovot. Some individuals in the city were distressed at his great success and chose a reprehensible means of getting rid of him. They circulated malicious slander in the media about him.*

Representatives of the Hamodia *newspaper wanted to print a response. Rav Kluft simply said, "It is better to say nothing."*

"But it is necessary to prevent a chillul Hashem!*"*

Again Rabbi Kluft said, "It is better to say nothing." He absolutely forbade any response.

He left the city in shame and humiliation and moved to Haifa. There he became not only Rav of Haifa, but the Rav of the entire Galil.

INSPIRATION

How did Lot become Avrohom's heir? Because he remained silent when Avrohom passed off Sorah as his sister. None of his actions brought him this reward — it was simply his silence, which saved the life of his uncle and the honor of his aunt. (Rashi on *Devarim* 2:5)

Speaking out would have been a depraved act from which he would have gained nothing. Why then did he receive such a sizeable reward? To teach us the significance of not speaking out.

(*Netzach Ha'Torah*, Chapter 2)

Reward For Guarding One's Tongue

According to the Vilna Gaon, the primary merit for gaining entrance into the World to Come is by guarding one's tongue. This is greater than all of the Torah study and good deeds that one performs. "By restraining one's speech, he merits the light hidden away for the righteous in the World to Come." (*Iggeres Ha'Gra*; *The Vilna Gaon*, page 139)

Rav Segal wrote that he had never seen someone who learned two laws of *shemiras ha'lashon* each day who had not merited a *yeshua* — whether it was being granted children, a *shidduch*, good health, *parnassah*, or success in the area of *chinuch*. He promised that whoever learned the laws would have the Chofetz Chaim as his advocate in heaven.

Rebbetzin Kanievsky has been advising numerous people to adopt this practice, and many of them have merited salvation.

Rebbetzin Kanievsky told her brother-in-law the following story, which is recorded in Borchi Nafshi, Shemos.

A fifteen-year-old girl was critically injured in a car accident. When the rescue crew arrived on the scene she was in a coma. The parents hurried to Bnai Brak to beg Rav Chaim and the Rebbetzin to daven for their daughter.

Two weeks passed, filled with countless prayers. And then the girl opened her eyes.

"How long was I asleep?' she asked her mother.

"Two weeks," her mother replied.

A look of concern crossed the daughter's face. "A few months ago I undertook to learn two halachos of shemiras ha'lashon *daily. I need to know how far I am behind and how much I need to do to catch up."*

The Kanievskys were thrilled to hear of her recovery. The Rebbetzin promised the parents that she would dance at their daughter's wedding.

Miraculously, the girl recovered completely, with no memento of her close call with death. Three years later she married an exceptional boy. The Rebbetzin attributed it all to the girl's commitment to study the laws of shemiras ha'lashon.

A person elevates his spiritual status and protects his soul from sin by muzzling his mouth (*Even Shleimah*, Chapter 7). Hashem becomes his protector and defense attorney (*Zachor Le'Miriam*, Chapter 3), and he merits a special place in the World to Come (*Chovas Ha'shemirah*, Chapter 5).

INSPIRATION

"And Shmuel grew up and Hashem was with him, and did not let any of his words fall to the ground" (*I Shmuel* 3:19). Hashem was with him because he was very careful about what he said.

(Be'er Moshe)

When a person restrains himself from speaking disparagingly of his fellow and arousing bad feeling toward him, the Accuser is unable to open his mouth.

Hashem is the source of goodness and compassion. He wishes to supply us with endless benefits. Even when we create destructive angels with our wicked deeds, Hashem desires that they not bear witness against us, for if they testify He will be obligated to punish us. (*Shabbos* 55a) If a person refuses to accept any negative reports about others, Hashem activates the "*middah k'negged middah* – measure for measure" principle and does not accept the testimony of destructive angels.

When Amatzya defamed Amos, Yeravam son of Yoash immediately rose to his defense (Amos 7:10–11). Yeravam, King of Yisroel, was rewarded for refusing to accept lashon hara *against Amos. Hashem enabled him to capture extensive territories that Yehoshua bin Nun and David Ha'melech were unable to capture.*

(Tanna De'bei Eliyahu Zuta 7; Reishis Chochmah, Shaar Ha'kedushah)

∘ ∘

EXERCISE

Take the time to master the art of listening. When listening to someone, look directly at the speaker and try to concentrate on his words. Signal your agreement when appropriate and state your disagreement as gently as possible. If you are being asked a question, wait a bit before answering. Show that you're giving thought to the question and fully considering your answers before speaking.

∘ ∘

When the tzaddik Rav Yehoshua Temoshvar visited Hungary he arranged to spend some time with Reb Chaim, a childless chassid who had been married for a few years. The tzaddik told him that he would like to come to his house for a meal. Honored by the impending visit, Reb Chaim prepared a festive meal and invited other respected people of the city to take part.

During the meal the tzaddik spoke words of Torah. At the end of the meal, the tzaddik remarked, "When people spend time together without uttering any *lashon hara, they have the power to expunge all bad decrees."*

He then turned and blessed Reb Chaim. His blessing was quickly fulfilled.

(*Purity of Speech*, lesson 41)

Another practical benefit of avoiding negative speech is that others will not speak *lashon hara* to you!

When Rebbetzin Ettel Kamenetsky would enter a room, all those present would stop speaking lashon hara.

(Reb Yaakov)

Against Ourselves

When we speak *lashon hara* we hurt ourselves. At the moment a person utters words of *lashon hara*, the Heavenly angels announce his own sins (*Rokeach*). It's like pulling in the prosecutor and handing him notes to use against you.

When a man speaks badly of others the angels recall his evil deeds and speak badly of him. Because he zeroed in on others' sins with a magnifying glass, the *beis din* up above will magnify his sins. (*Einei Yitzchok, Archin* 16)

From a practical standpoint, people will keep a distance from someone whose conversation is loaded with *lashon hara*. His friends feel they cannot trust him, for someone who cannot muzzle his mouth will be tempted to share their confidences with others. Even potential business associates will be wary of dealing with a person who evaluates others in a bad light and then passes his opinions on to others.

When a person is not careful to avoid speaking *lashon hara,* it is an indication that he does not fear the punishment of the Heavenly Court — or even that he does not believe that Hashem has commanded us to avoid speaking ill of others. (*Zachor Le'Miriam*, Chapter 14)

A lawyer once pointed out a court building in Manhattan where people accused of serious crimes are brought to justice. He related that after sitting in on a case of that nature and witnessing the fear and uneasiness that pervade the courtroom, one could easily conceptualize the severity of the judgment that we will be subject to after 120 years in this world. Certainly we would want to avail ourselves of all possible help to emerge innocent at that crucial defining moment, when our eternal existence is being determined!

INSPIRATION

In the famous letter of instruction the Vilna Gaon gave his family when he left for Eretz Yisroel, he wrote, "In the Next World, for each vain word that he spoke, a person is punished by being slung from one end of the universe to the other. This is merely for unnecessary words. But regarding forbidden matters such as slander, scoffing, oaths and vows, controversy, and curses—particularly in the shul and on Shabbos and holidays—for these one must descend deep into Sheol. And one's every single word has been recorded."

When the Chofetz Chaim was in Vienna, he davened with a private minyan for two weeks. Everyone he encountered was struck by his simplicity. Once, after davening Shacharis, he spoke to his minyan and explained the severity of the sin of lashon hara. *"Every sin breeds an accusing angel which is mute. Lashon hara, however, breeds a prosecuting angel with the power of speech, making the sin of* lashon hara *worse than all others."*

(*Siach Zekeinim*, Vol. III, page 401)

A man once spoke lashon hara *in the Chofetz Chaim's presence. The Chofetz Chaim tried to stop him, but could not. With a sigh, the Chofetz Chaim exclaimed, "For* lashon hara *one's tongue is severed."*

Not long afterward the man had to have his tongue surgically removed.

(Told by Rav Yisroel Yaakov Lubchansky, who was present; *Kuntrus Peh Kadosh*)

The *yetzer hara* strives to induce us to speak *lashon hara* to defile our mouths. He wants nothing better than to block our *tefillos*.

Food For Thought

"There are a number of accusers whose task is to seize any bad word or foul word that a person brings forward from his mouth; and when he later brings forth holy words, woe unto them, woe unto their lives. Woe to them in This World, woe to them in the World to Come. Because these defiled spiritual beings take that defiled word, and when the person later brings forth holy words, those defiled spiritual beings ... defile the holy words, so they bring no merit to him and the strength of the holiness is weakened."

(*Zohar*)

The two great chassidic giants, Reb Nachman of Breslov and the Shpoler Zeide, were embroiled in conflict. How did this great controversy come about?

The Zeide had a relative who never spoke, from fear of uttering lashon hara. *After twenty-eight years, he finally broke his silence — by speaking out against Reb Nachman, thus starting the conflict.*

Sighed Reb Nachman, "Brothers, look how powerful the temptation of lashon hara *is. For twenty-eight years the evil inclination kept that fellow silent, just so his* lashon hara *would be believed."*

A father's great love for his child impels him to make allowances for bad behavior. But when people report the child's bad behavior in specific detail, the father is forced to take strong measures to ensure that the child mends his ways.

We are all Hashem's children. No father wants to hear his children portrayed in a negative way. When we paint someone in a negative light because of what we consider inappropriate behavior, we are ignoring the fact that in Hashem's eyes, he is still a precious Jewish soul. The speaker of *lashon hara* counters Hashem's greatest desire, depriving Hashem of *nachas* from His children. (*Meor Einayim, Parshas Metzorah*)

When Rav Levi Yitzchok of Berditchev heard someone speaking badly about another, he would reprove him. "I don't understand how you are not afraid to speak ill about Hashem's own tefillin. According to the Midrash, *Hashem wears tefillin that says, 'Umi ke'amcha Yisroel — who is like Your people Israel!'"*

Food For Thought

There is a certain spiritual being who is in charge of those who habitually speak *lashon hara*. A defiled spiritual being ... he rests on the arousal of *lashon hara* and comes up above and causes death, war and killing.

(Zohar)

If a person seals his mouth against *lashon hara*, gossip, falsehood, and offensive speech, then he has the right to say, "My father, my king, seal the mouths of those who hate us and lobby against us."

(Chofetz Chaim, *Chovas Ha'shemirah*)

Destroying Others

If only people were more conscious of the tragic consequences of hurting someone with speech! There are so many people who study the laws of *shemiras ha'lashon*, but don't grasp the serious import of the prohibition against inflicting pain on someone else.

The speaker of *lashon hara* reasons to himself that he has done nothing serious: "What are a few words, after all?" Since his conscience is clear, there is nothing to deter him from continuing on his ill-fated path of gossipmongering. The outcome of this phenomenon is that while murderers are few, speakers of *lashon hara* are unfortunately many.

Food For Thought

"Each Jew is obligated to pursue peace and bind his fellow Jews to one another with strands of love. This is the only way to augment the vigor of our people. It is understood that one must avoid sowing hate and conflict through *lashon hara*, which poisons our spirits and arouses evil currents that result in our being subject to the swords of our enemies, who will batter us and embitter our lives."
(Rav Aharon Levin, *Ha'derash Ve'ha'iyun Metzorah* 124)

"Woe to those who set their eyes on something and have no idea what they are observing. People experience setbacks and crises and assign the blame to external forces. They curse the perceived starting points: the anti-Semite, the Arab, the pollution, the economy. They don't realize that the cause of all the death lies elsewhere, as it says, 'Life and death are in the hands of the tongue.' "
(Klausenberger Rebbe, *Parshas Va'eirah* 5748)

Several laborers were given plots of land to cultivate. But at the end of the day, not one had done the job correctly. Many had planted, but did not properly weed the garden. Yes, some had more weeds, and some had less; but all the fields appeared neglected. Would any of them have the temerity to criticize the work of another to the man who had hired them?

We know how difficult it is for each of us to accomplish our tasks, and how much encouragement we require to keep moving ahead. Knowing this increases the foolishness of zeroing in on another's faults. Why focus on the failures of others when we can focus on their accomplishments?

(*Ahavas Meisharim*)

Food For Thought

Speaking badly about any Jew is like being critical of Hashem, for each Jew has a portion of Hashem within. When one speaks in a negative fashion about a Jew, that G-dly portion is also included.

(*Shearis Yisroel*)

A person who spends time chatting will inevitably speak *lashon hara*. He may start speaking about neighbors, but eventually he will speak badly of righteous scholars, and ultimately of the Creator Himself.

(*Kad Ha'kemach*, Letter *lamed*)

"You shall not go about as a peddler in your nation" (*Parshas Kedoshim*). The word for peddler, *rachil*, is written with an unnecessary letter *yud*. This is because the peddler of gossip inevitably transgresses the Ten Commandments.

(*Baal Ha'turim*)

Often we have no idea of the harm that words can cause. Although the victim of *lashon hara* does not suffer bodily harm, he may suffer more than if he had been physically abused. Cuts and bruises heal, but the humiliation and shame from *lashon hara* can leave deep emotional scars that might never heal.

Money can be recovered, but a good name developed over years can be wiped away instantly by *lashon hara*. Depending on the circumstances it may be nearly impossible to fully restore the person's reputation.

> *Rav Dov Berish Rosenberg, the Rav of Strikov, cried out in his Shabbos Ha'gadol derasha, "Weeks before Pesach, people come to me with all sorts of involved questions regarding the koshering of various household items and the kashrus of certain foods. Why, then, does no one ask me the most important question, 'How shall we insert the holy matzoh into our mouths, the mouths that we have defiled throughout the year with* lashon hara, *falsehood, and other forbidden forms of speech? How shall we kasher our mouths?'"*
>
> *All who were present burst into bitter weeping.*

Food For Thought

The snake was asked what benefit it receives when it bites someone. The snake replied, "Before asking me that question, ask the same question of the speakers of *lashon hara*."

The snake was then asked why he bites one part of the body, but his poison spreads all over. The snake replied, "Before you ask me that question, ask those who speak *lashon hara* why they stand in Rome and kill in Syria, stand in Syria and kill in Rome."

(*Devarim Rabbah* 5)

A gunshot cannot kill out of the gun's range, but *lashon hara* can cause havoc throughout the world. A word spoken in Chicago can result in someone in Eretz Yisroel losing a job. A thoughtless conversation in Yerushalayim can break up a *shidduch* in Los Angeles. An e-mail written in New York can cause humiliation and embarrassment in London.

Hurtful words can also destroy a marriage.

Rav Meshulam Igra was known for his brilliance. Even in a generation of great luminaries he stood out.

He married the daughter of a very wealthy man. Some people living in his father-in-law's city were jealous of the young man, and they spoke badly of him to his father-in-law. They succeeded so well that the man decided to arrange a divorce for his daughter from the ne'er-do-well she had married.

Several years later there was a halachic issue that many of the generation's greatest minds were grappling with. The Gaon Rav Yeshaya Pick, author of Mesores Ha'Shas, *received an excellent treatment of the issue from someone who signed himself "Meshulam Igra." When he read the discussion written by this young scholar, Rav Pick was deeply impressed by his breadth, depth, and orderly thinking.*

Rav Yeshaya Pick was determined to discover the identity of this young genius. He happened to encounter a wealthy man who lived in the same city as Rav Meshulam Igra, and he asked the man if he knew "the brilliant gaon, Rav Meshulam Igra," who lived in his area.

When the rich man heard the question, he fainted. After reviving him, Rav Yeshaya Pick asked what had caused him to faint.

"This gaon was my son-in-law, and I convinced my daughter to divorce him and threw him out of my house," the wealthy man lamented.

"If that is the case," Rav Pick replied, "then you can faint again."

(*Mesoras Avos, Vayikra*)

Hurtful gestures can kill people.

A Torah scholar traveled abroad to collect funds to marry off his daughter. A wealthy philanthropist inquired about this scholar. The man he asked responded with a gesture, indicating that he couldn't fully give his stamp of approval. The scholar received no funds. He was so devastated that he fell ill and died in his prime.

(*Ohr Le'tziyon*)

Thoughtless words can destroy a person's business.

Rav Moshe Feinstein was eating breakfast together with a visitor. Rav Moshe reached for a container of milk, but appeared to have a change of heart and returned it to its place. He then reached for another carton of milk manufactured by another company and poured himself some milk.

The visitor concluded that Rav Moshe did not trust the manufacturer of the first container of milk. He decided that he would publicize what he had seen for the benefit of those who were careful about what they consumed.

In a short time the news spread to stores, schools, and hotels. Many people stopped dealing with that manufacturer. Hearing that the source of their troubles was Rav Moshe's opposition, the company owners paid him a visit in an attempt to discover why the Rav had ruled that their product was not fit for consumption.

When he heard their question, Rav Moshe was astonished. "Just this morning I had some of your milk."

The company owners offered enough details that Reb Moshe recalled the incident. A smile crossed his face as he remembered. "There was a simple reason that I returned your carton of milk to its place. It was empty!"

Reb Moshe immediately sat down to write a warm letter of endorsement for the milk company.

(Ve'ha'ish Moshe, Part II)

When a person's life comes to an end and he stands trial before the King of kings, he might find mitzvos on his record that he did not do during his lifetime. When he inquires as to the meaning of this apparent error, he will be told, "The mitzvos of all who spoke *lashon hara* about you were transferred to your record." He will also find that some *aveiros* he committed are gone, for they have been transferred to the person who spoke badly of him.

Unfortunately, he may also find sins that he never committed. He will be informed that the sins of those about whom he spoke negatively are now on his record. (*Chovos Ha'levavos*; *Shemiras Ha'lashon, Shaar Ha'zechirah*, Chapter 7; *Ziporen Shamir* 13:216)

It is important to note that the number of merits and sins transferred is according to the weight and intents of the *lashon hara* spoken. Measure for measure, to the extent that the speaker wants to degrade the one spoken about — to that extent his own stature is lowered. (*Yad Dovid*)

A person who does not control his speech is therefore unable to keep track of his deeds for spiritual reckoning. He has no idea of the sum total of his virtues and shortcomings. (Rav Yosef Salant, *Be'er Yosef*)

Being burdened with unknown sins means that repentance is beyond his reach. It is true that if one commits a similar sin and repents sincerely, he eradicates sins of the same nature. But his personality and character may be completely dissimilar to the person whose sins he acquired, and he may never perpetrate an analogous sin. (Rav Raphael Ha'Kohein of Hamburg)

The only solution? To sincerely repent for the sin of speaking *lashon hara*.

INSPIRATION

When a person repents for having spoken *lashon hara* his mitzvos are returned to him (*Chovos Ha'levavos*). This is the explanation of the use of the future tense in the verse, "This shall be the law of the *metzorah* on the day of his purification" (*Vayikra* 14:2). When the speaker of *lashon hara* who was punished with *tzara'as* repents and is purified, his Torah will be restored to him so he can call it his own.

(*Divrei Yoel, Parshas Metzorah*)

Rav Yehudah Tzadkah once interrupted a boy during a siyum, *in the middle of the* hadran *as he was saying, "May Torah be your profession in This World and remain with you in the World to Come."*

The Rav asked, "Isn't it understood that one will enjoy the rewards of one's Torah in the World to Come?"

Rav Tzadkah then offered the answer to his question. "Unfortunately, this may not always be the case, for when a person speaks lashon hara *his achievements will be acquired by someone else."*

(*Ve'zos Le'Yehudah*)

A righteous man became aware that lashon hara *had been spoken about him. Instead of becoming angry, he sent the perpetrator a gift with a note. "You sent me your mitzvos as a gift and I would like to reciprocate."*

(*Chovos Ha'levavos, ShaarHa'keniah*, Chapter 7;
Orchos Tzaddikim, Shaar Ha'anavah)

Rabbeinu Dovid Ha'nagid, grandson of the Rambam, tells a similar story of a Torah scholar in his community.

(Commentary to *Avos*)

When we speak *lashon hara* we lead others to sin. A person who is responsible for influencing other to transgress is considered worse than a murderer.

Food For Thought

Know that a person who constantly speaks *lashon hara* has shed much blood.

(*Shevet Mussar*)

Moshe Rabbeinu could not understand the reason the Jewish People were forced to suffer so much. When he became aware of the slanderous reports of Dasan and Aviram, everything became clear to him. (*Shemos Rabbah, Parshah* 1)

When Rabi Yosi son of Chalafta was a youngster he played with the other youngsters. A man saw him and said, "I will tell your father that you are playing with the youngsters."

Rabi Yosi replied, "Why would you do that? If you tell my father he will hit me, and you will get your tongue used to speaking lashon hara.*"*

(*Midrash Tehillim 3*)

On some occasions *lashon hara* can kill a fourth individual. When Doeg spoke *lashon hara*, Shaul, who listened to his evil words, was slain; Achimelech, who was spoken about, was killed; and so was Doeg. Avner also was killed as a result, because he could have spoken up to prevent the *lashon hara* from being accepted but did not. (*Midrash Sheloshim U'shtayim Middos*)

> *A man visiting the Imrei Emes once began speaking negatively about a third person. The Rebbe rebuked the man subtly but harshly for his lack of discretion.*
>
> *"The* Gemara *teaches that one who humiliates his friend in the presence of a* talmid chacham *is considered a heretic [Sanhedrin 99b]. I can't imagine that you consider yourself a heretic, so it must be that you don't consider me a* talmid chacham. *I must ask you, therefore — did you really go through all the trouble and expense of coming to see me just to hint to me that I am not a* talmid chacham?"
>
> (*Rosh Golas Ariel*)

The Temptation Of *Lashon Hara*

Why do people speak *lashon hara*?

Some people are simply very talkative. A man sits with his friend, chatting and exchanging opinions about family, teachers and more. Others just like to know everything and comment on everyone. They lack the ability to hold back. (*Ohr Le'tziyon*)

Often a person speaks *lashon hara* because of his desire to feel important. When people share a juicy bit of gossip, all eyes are on them and they are the center of attention. The motivation for the listener is often similar. He feels flattered by the attention of the speaker and by the fact that the latter considers him trustworthy enough to receive this important piece of information.

But these positive feelings are illusory and short-lived.

> *An unsavory character took to the streets one day, dressed in a fashionable manner that suggested a position of prominence and wealth. Noticing an out of town guest, the man greeted the visitor warmly and expressed his willingness to help the other with anything he might need.*
>
> *After showing him the sights of the town, the graceful host offered to treat the visitor to a meal at one of the city's posh restaurants. "Please order whatever your heart desires," he chirped. "The cost is of no concern whatsoever."*
>
> *After the two had eaten a delicious repast, the con man stealthily crept out of the restaurant. When it came time to pay, the hapless visitor had no choice but to foot the bill for both portions.*
>
> *This* mashal, *says the Chofetz Chaim, aptly describes what happens when one relates* lashon hara *to another, satisfying their desire for juicy, savory morsels of gossip. But when the time to pay comes in the Next World, the listener will feel nothing but hostility and animosity toward the one who fed him serious* aveiros!
>
> (*The Magic Elixir*)

A person will speak *lashon hara* to tear down someone else, which propels the speaker to a higher notch. The worse he paints the life of another, he thinks, the better he himself appears. Instead of affirming his own value independently, he believes his value is affirmed by putting down others.

> *Someone came to visit the Chofetz Chaim's home and spend some time talking with family members. When he left, one of the members of the family repeated something about the guest that was not so complimentary.*
>
> *The Chofetz Chaim declared, "I don't want to hear anyone speaking badly of others! I have enough of my own deficiencies to deal with and talk about ..."*
>
> *The speaker attempted to justify himself. "The visitor himself told us this. Apparently he felt comfortable sharing the information."*
>
> *The Chofetz Chaim replied, "A person may not react to a self-inflicted slap, but he will be deeply hurt when others slap him."*
>
> (*Mayim Chayim, Kedoshim*)

Food For Thought

There is no cheaper high for self-importance addicts than trivializing and belittling others. It gives such people the feeling of superiority without any need to actually be superior.

(Rebbetzin Tzipporah Heller)

A distinguished Rebbetzin in Yerushalayim was sitting on the bus in front of two young ladies. These two students were engrossed in a conversation concerning one of their peers, who had just become engaged the previous night. In a manner unbecoming such intelligent and frum *girls, they proceeded to dissect the other girl in an inappropriate fashion. By the time they had completed their dissection, the only conclusion that remained was their expression of pity for the unfortunate* chassan.

The Rebbetzin could not help overhearing the negative comments, and decided to teach them a lesson. She turned around and said, "I couldn't help listening to your conversation. I cannot thank you enough for your frank description of this girl. You see, I am the mother of the chassan *to whom your friend is engaged. When I return home, I am going to have a serious talk with my son and insist that he call off the engagement. This is not the type of girl I want my son to marry."*

The girls were shocked and horrified. They had never intended their friend any real harm! They were probably just envious of her — and envy invariably leads to slander and worse. What could they do now to dissuade the woman from taking this fateful step? Was there any way to undo the harm they had caused?

The two girls learned a profound lesson about the tragic effects of lashon hara.

(Rav Yitzchok Zilberstein)

Some people consider chewing over other people's bad behavior a pleasurable pastime. Others will speak lashon hara out of boredom. How sad — people entertain themselves and overcome their own emptiness by destroying the lives of others.

INSPIRATION

When the righteous delight, there is much praise [spoken]. But when the wicked arise, men's [faults] are ferreted out." (*Mishlei* 28:12) Rabbeinu Yonah explains that it is the "tendency of wicked people to focus on the faults of others, while tzaddikim look for opportunities to praise people's virtues. (*Shaarei Teshuvah* 1:18) Why is this so?

When one acknowledges the good deeds of others, it places a demand on him to make similar efforts to do good. On the other hand, when he dwells on the negative side of human behavior, he placates his conscience with the attitude that no one is really living up to expectations, so he needn't feel so bad about his own shortcomings. Thus speaking *lashon hara* enables us to avoid taking life seriously.

The Vilna Gaon suggested that to overcome the desire to speak *lashon hara* a person must habituate himself to praising others. (*The Vilna Gaon,* page 140)

The *yetzer hara* will try to convince a person that what he wants to say is not *lashon hara*. He will even claim that it is a mitzvah to publicize the deeds of that individual.

Food for Thought

The Alter Rebbe explained the passage from the *Hagaddah*: " '*Rasha mahu*' — what the wicked man's [nature] is '*Omer*' — he conveys to others."

(*Naos Deshe*) "*Vas me redt, redt man auf sich* — what a person utters reflects on himself."

(*The Brisker Rav*)

Punishment For Listening To *Lashon Hara*

Why is the punishment for one who listens, a passive participant, greater than the one who actively speaks the derogatory words? The listener has the power to change the course of the conversation. Rav Mordechai Schwab explains that the listener commits a more insidious act than the speaker, for he wraps up and complements the speaker's act of aggression. The speaker initiates the sin; the listener completes it. Without the listener, the speaker's words would have no essence, no substance, nowhere to go, because no one would be listening. If there is no listener, there is no *lashon hara*. Thus, the listener commits the greater act of malevolence.

> *When the firstborn were killed In Egypt, the dogs controlled themselves and did not growl or whine. Hashem endowed man with intellect and sense, yet this person is unable to control himself and refuse to listen to the slanderer. He is therefore even lower than a dog.*
>
> (Maharal as cited by the Chofetz Chaim)

One who accepts evil speech deserves being thrown to the dogs. Those who speak *lashon hara* will often be reincarnated as dogs. Even worse, they will suffer terribly from the memory that they were previously human beings. (*Chareidim*, Chapter 33)

Food For Thought

When a person hears *lashon hara* spoken about a Torah scholar, it is not enough to refuse to believe it—he must actively rise to the defense of the scholar spoken about. One who doesn't do so will be punished.

(*Menoras Ha'maor*)

A worried young father told Rav Chaim Moshe Mandel that his child was persistently coming down with terrible ear infections. The doctors had given up on him. What should he do?

Rav Mandel advised that the father should undertake to avoid listening to lashon hara *and* rechilus. *The young man took his recommendation very seriously and implemented this advice immediately. From that moment on the infections totally disappeared.*

(*Harav Mandel*)

The *Talmud* in *Shabbos* 56a quotes Rav as stating that David Ha'melech accepted a slanderous report. After David established his monarchy, he sought out descendants of Shaul Ha'melech, so he could honor them out of his desire to pay tribute to Yehonasan, Shaul's son. The king discovered a slave named Tziva from the house of Shaul. He, in turn, informed David that one son of Yehonasan, called Mefiboshes, was still alive.

Tziva intimated that Mefiboshes was devoid of Torah knowledge. David Ha'Melech later discovered that Mefiboshes was a Torah scholar. Even though David realized that Tziva had slandered Mefiboshes, at a later date he still approached him to inquire about Mefiboshes's whereabouts. When Tziva told David Ha'melech that Mefiboshes had committed treason, he believed those slanderous words and gave Mefiboshes's property to Tziva.

Chazal say that David was punished *middah k'neged middah*, measure for measure. Since he believed slander and divided Mefiboshes's property between master (Mefiboshes) and slave (Tziva), Hashem divided David's kingdom between king (Rechavam) and servant (Yeravam).

This act ultimately prevented the Jewish People from making their pilgrimage to Yerushalayim. Our present exile indirectly has its roots in this episode where a derogatory implication was accepted about someone.

No participation, no speaking, just listening. The result: *galus*, exile. Do we need to hear more?

Food For Thought

For three sins a person is punished in this world, while the remainder is reserved for the World to Come. *Lashon hara* is the equivalent of all three.

(*Reishis Chochmah, Shaar Ha'kedushah*)

Avoiding *Lashon Hara*

To gossip is a bad habit, and bad habits can be broken. Each person must decide on ways and means that will enable him to avoid speaking *lashon hara*. There are generic rules that most people find beneficial, while some tools are suitable for specific individuals or specific situations. There are certain to be some techniques that suit our personality.

> *Rav Yitzchok Ariel was known for his avoidance of* lashon hara. *He would regularly study the halachos of* shemiras ha'lashon *and was always seeking ways and means of preventing the speaking of* lashon hara *in his environment.*
>
> *One way he would break up a group engaged in inappropriate conversation was to call the speaker aside and ask him if he could tell him what time it was. He would raise his wristwatch to eye level so the slanderer would see the words, "Remember what was done to Miriam," taped to the face of his watch. Another technique was to approach the maligner and say to him, "It is important to record your statement," and he would hand him a pen in a way that he would see the fateful words on his watch.*
>
> *When smaller reminders failed, he would give the habitual offender a beautiful gift: a copy of the book* Shemiras Ha'lashon *by the Chofetz Chaim.*
>
> *(Gevuras Yitzchok)*

> *Rav Yosef Dov Ha'levi Soloveitchik was seen opening his container of snuff during a conversation and*

glancing inside. It was later discovered that he had in-scribed the letters shin, peh, vav, shin, mem, *and* nun *inside the container. These were meant to remind him of the words:* "**S**homer **P**iv **U**'le'shono **S**homer **M**e'tzaras **N**afsho—*Guarding one's mouth and tongue [is the equivalent] of guarding one's self from suffering.*"

All About Attitude

There is generally no correlation between our attitude to-wards a sin and its actual severity. Our mindset is actually fashioned by the number of times we see the sin committed. A person will usually be very disturbed to see a Jew eating chicken with milk (forbidden by our Sages), but will not re-act with equal distress when hearing someone speaking *lashon hara* (forbidden by the Torah).

> *I remember when a young grandson of mine ob-served a man get out of a car on Shabbos and then put a yarmulke on his head and enter a shul. He was so horrified that he couldn't stop talking about it. The reason adults do not react in this fashion is be-cause we have witnessed so much* chillul Shabbos, Rachmana litzlan.

> *A Rav visited the Chofetz Chaim to consult with him. At first the two began a discussion relating to their studies, as is the wont of Torah scholars on meet-ing. Then the Rav said, "Now let us move on to* lashon hara," *intending to present his questions relating to* shemiras ha'lashon.

The Chofetz Chaim nearly fainted. To him the Rav could have just as well said, "Now let us have some ham."

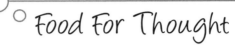

Food For Thought

If a person makes the effort to speak less *lashon hara* weekly, even if he speaks just ten less words a day, this will add up to three thousand words of *lashon hara* avoided each year. He has thus created three thousand angels who will advocate on his behalf.

(*Kiddushin* 39)

Judging Favorably

Training oneself not to speak derogatorily about one's fellow Jews requires a complete reorientation in how we view other people. Once we have made an unfavorable judgment in our own mind of another's character or behavior, the impulse to verbally express that judgment is often almost irresistible. To avoid speaking negatively about others, then, we first have to learn how to judge them favorably.

Learning Halachos

Studying the halachos and *hashkofos* of *shmiras ha'lashon* is an effective tool for self control, and actually shrinks our desire to speak *lashon hara*. (Rav Betzalel Ha'kohein of Vilna) The *yetzer hara* always suggests that the forbidden is permitted. If a person is convinced that a forbidden statement is not *lashon hara*, or that it is permitted to make that statement, then his good intention will not help. One must first know what is actually considered *lashon hara*.

Learning the laws will prevent a person from falling into the category of a regular speaker of *lashon hara*. Another advantage of familiarizing oneself with all the halachos is that a person who is aware that he has sinned can do *teshuvah*.

Food For Thought

If a person hasn't mastered the halachos of *shmiras ha'lashon* he is best limiting his speaking.

(Klausenberger Rebbe)

Loving Others

If we truly believe that all Jews are part of one unit, we would not speak badly about others (*Techeles Mordechai*). Contemplation on the G-dly essence of every individual leads one to love every Jew. Gradually, we will begin reaching out to others in a positive way. (*Areshes Sefaseinu*)

What greater *segulah* for Hashem's favor than not speaking badly about Hashem's children? (*Chofetz Chaim*)

> *A group of young men learning in Yeshivas Hevron wanted to start studying the work* Chofetz Chaim. *They came to the* mashgiach, *Rav Meir Chadash, to get his blessing.*

He told them, "Have you ever encountered a son who speaks badly about a beloved father or brother, or a friend he is greatly attached to? If there is a need to say something, he will invest great effort in researching what is permissible and what is forbidden. And if he heard someone speaking unfavorably about these cherished individuals, he would immediately put a stop to the conversation.

"It appears, then, that if one shares or listens to negative information about another, he must not value that individual."

The mashgiach *therefore advised that they begin by studying the sources that stress Hashem's love for His children. Then they should turn their attention to studying about our obligation to love our fellow Jew and desire that only good befall them.*

Practice Makes Perfect

The longer one persists in guarding one's tongue, the easier it is. It becomes more natural to weigh your words more carefully.

Set aside time daily to consider if you have been careful about avoiding speaking negatively about others (*Chovas Ha'shemirah*, Introduction). "If a day passes and a person has not picked up on the need to repent for something he said, it is an indication that his soul is unrefined — unless he is on the level of the Chofetz Chaim" (Letter of Rav Yitzchok Ariel). After a sin, the sensitized soul feels the distressing feeling of being detached from Hashem.

The Chofetz Chaim was observed in intense conversation with a chassidic Rebbe at an important meeting. A listener later related what he heard:

The Chofetz Chaim pleaded to be exempt from attending the next meeting. The Rebbe asked, "Why don't you want to attend?"

The Chofetz Chaim responded, "From my youth, I always tried to keep away from saying anything negative about people. I know there will be discussions about candidates and there is a possibility that negative comments will surface in reference to the candidates."

The Rebbe questioned, "But what about your city, Radin? Surely there have been community meetings relating to choosing the Rav and other community officials."

The Chofetz Chaim explained, "That's why I left the city at the exact time that they were choosing a Rav, so I could not be asked to join the meeting. By the time I came back, the new Rav had already been appointed."

Hearing those words had a dramatic effect on those present and impressed a lasting lesson on their hearts.

(*Meir Einei Yisroel*)

EXERCISE

Speaking badly of others is a very revealing form of projection. What you don't like about yourself, you tend to point out in others. When you find yourself critical of others, take a moment to consider your guilt in the area you find so offensive.

When you are about to say something about someone, stop and ask yourself if you would say it in their presence.

(*Orchos Yosher*, Chapter 4)

● ●

Avoid Hearing *Lashon Hara*

There are always three sides to any conflict: his side, her side, and the truth. Even if the speaker sounds like he or she has all the facts right and claims to have a first-person account of all events, your obligation is to not believe what is being said.

● ●

EXERCISE

When someone blurts out something that is *lashon hara*, repeat to yourself, "I don't believe it. I don't believe it." This should be followed by, "There is another side, there is another side."

● ●

A man once came to Rabbi Eliyahu Dushnitzer and began to complain about a terrible injustice that had been done to him by a certain individual. Rav Eliyahu appeared to be listening, and never once did he interrupt the speaker.

When the man finished, Rav Eliyahu said to him, "I want you to know that I do not believe anything you just said. The reason I did not interrupt you is because I understand your anguish, and I wanted you to get it out of your system. I was worried that if I could not succeed in calming you down, you would tell your story to others who might believe your lashon hara. *In that case, you would have sinned and caused others to sin. I repeat, I do not and will not believe what you have said."*

(*Nachlas Eliyahu*)

If you are at a *simchah* and walk over to a group of ladies who are in the middle of speaking *lashon hara*, keep walking. If you cannot walk away (for example, because you are in a moving vehicle), you are obligated to take your mind elsewhere. Think about anything other than what is actually being said. You can plan your dinner, think about a problem that needs your attention, and drift into dreamland.

Never allow yourself to be drawn into a conversation about a group of individuals, for how will you ever attain forgiveness for such a sin?

Rabbi Shlomo Leib of Lentchna was orphaned from both his parents when he was very young. The good people of his city arranged for him to sleep in the home of the local tailor.

The room where the young Reb Shlomo Leib slept was really part of the tailor's workroom, separated by a curtain. He could hear the tailor's conversations with his assistants, which often included lashon hara *and mockery. Shlomo Leib decided to*

remain in the beis medrash *until the tailor's work-*
day was over, so he would not hear any forbidden
conversation.

One evening when Shlomo Leib arrived at the
tailor's home, he heard loud voices emanating from
the workroom. It was Erev Yom Tov, and the tailor
had decided to stay later than usual to complete the
many Yom Tov orders.

The wind blew fiercely as young Shlomo Leib
huddled outside, shivering with cold. The thought of
his warm bed was tempting, but the child would not
come in until the light in the tailor's room was out.

Some possible things you might want to say to prevent
someone from sharing *lashon hara* with you:

- "Do you think that might be *lashon hara*?"
- "Maybe she wouldn't want me to know this."
- "If someone said that about you, you wouldn't want
  me to listen."
- "If someone said that about you I would feel terrible."
- "Maybe she had a reason we don't relate to or don't
  know for doing what she did."
- "You weren't there, and didn't hear it yourself. Therefore you can't know the real truth. If you were there
  you might have seen it differently."
- "You know so much about [a certain concept]. Please
  share some of your knowledge with me. I'm always
  learning so much from you."
- When you cannot prevent someone from speaking *lashon
  hara*, explain the concept of *Machsom Le'fi*. Tell them

that it is your hours for not speaking *lashon hara.*

- Try changing the topic with, "Oh what a beautiful ring!" or "I must tell you something very important before I forget!" You might choose to jump in with an exciting announcement, a financial prediction — anything that distracts the speaker so the conversation is directed elsewhere.
- Try excusing yourself: "I just remembered I need to take care of something. I'd better go now."

Trying to avoid temptation when your friend turns to you with some juicy gossip? Consider these:

- Reflect on the fact that today your friend is talking about a mutual acquaintance; but tomorrow it will likely be you!
- Visualize the person being spoken about on their hands and knees, begging you not to speak badly about them (Rav Yechezkel Levenstein). It has been strongly recommended that one repeat this exercise on a regular basis (Rav Mattisyahu Salomon).
- Visualize how the person speaking words of *lashon hara* to you will one day say, "You knew what a terrible sin *lashon hara* is; why didn't you stop me?"

- -

EXERCISE

When you have inadvertently heard *lashon hara* you must say to yourself, "I refuse to accept this statement as true."

Repeat to yourself, "I feel terrible that another person was belittled."

- -

Rav Itzele Peterburger was once in the company of people who spoke lashon hara. *He couldn't stop them, so he sang out with great feeling, "Al cheit shechatanu le'fanecha be'bitui sefasayim — for the sin we have sinned before you with the utterance of one's mouth" (*Vidui *prayer).*

(Kochvei Ohr)

Even if a person rejects *lashon hara* he has heard, there is usually some vestige of the negative report that remains with him. Remind yourself that many people lie and everyone exaggerates. Even when we personally observe an event, it can be difficult to determine the truth; certainly, secondhand information is very suspect. (*Le'Shichno Tidrishu*)

The following anecdote is an excellent depiction of this process:

A Rav once addressed the members of a shul on behalf of a well-known yeshivah. The congregation appeared to be very moved by his words. Suddenly, the speaker noted a drastic change in the audience. Respectful, interested expressions had been replaced by scornful stares. Those who had been hanging on every word now had a contemptuous look on their faces.

The Rav stopped speaking and asked, "Gentlemen, what accounts for this radical change?"

The shul's gabbai *rose. "We just found out that you were responsible for the theft of all the Torah scrolls in your city."*

The Rav did not lose his composure. "May I ask who was the source of that information?"

The gabbai *pointed to his friend sitting next to him. The friend rose and declared, "I didn't say that. I told him that you had stolen some Torah scrolls in your city, but I didn't say all."*

"Who informed you of that?" asked the Rav.

The man turned to the gentleman behind him, who loudly asserted, "I said only one Torah."

"And who was your source?" the Rav asked.

The man pointed to his comrade sitting at his side. "I didn't even mention a Sefer Torah,*" the comrade declared. "I told him that you had stolen some books."*

"Who told you that?" asked the Rav.

His reply was immediate. "Our rabbi's son."

The rabbi's son rose to defend himself. "He misunderstood. I only suggested that the Rav's lecture was stolen from a sefer. *That is how the story of the theft began."*

One piece of lashon hara *snowballed into a crushing indictment.*

(*Imrei Shefer*, part I)

The listener has the ability to stop evil speech in its tracks (*Bereishis Rabbah, Parshah* 20). When someone refuses to stop speaking *lashon hara*, show your disapproval — frown or look displeased. That will stop him from continuing. (*Reishis Chochmah, Shaar Ha'kedushah*)

The faster you stop him, the better. Each additional word is an additional *aveirah*.

Reb Zalman of Volozhin once chaired a meeting
of talmidei chachamim where the topic of conversation revolved around Torah topics. Each individual
offered his comments and insights, and enjoyed
hearing the words of his colleagues.

Suddenly, one of the men mentioned something
unrelated to Torah. His remarks bordered on lashon
hara. Rav Zalma'le immediately put his fingers over
his ears, quoting the Gemara in Kesubos that teaches
that one should place two fingers on his ears on
hearing lashon hara.

(Toldos Adom)

When Rav Yitzchok Elchonon Spector could not
prevent a group of prominent individuals from sharing a negative report, he would suddenly doze off.
When the conversation moved on to acceptable topics, he would suddenly awake.

(Toldos Yitzchok)

When Rabbi Shmuel Ha'daya moved to Yerushalayim, a lovely apartment was offered to him in the
Bucharim neighborhood. But Rav Shmuel expressed
a preference for living in the Ohel Moshe area. He
explained that because Arabic, his mother tongue,
was the common language spoken in the Bucharim
neighborhood, there was a greater chance that he
might stumble in terms of lashon hara. In Ohel

Moshe, Ladino was more commonly used, and Rav Shmuel was less familiar with that language. He would be able to live more peacefully there, without being as concerned about inadvertently being told lashon hara.

(*Be'shaarei Ha'lashon*)

Before Reb Refoel of Hamburg met with anyone wishing to discuss something with him, he would preface each conversation with, "Please let's not talk about anyone besides ourselves."

(*Samah De'chayei*)

Another practical way of avoiding *lashon hara* is to stay away from individuals who tend to readily speak *lashon hara*. Avoiding contact with these people is a step in the right direction.

Reb Zev lived in a small town in Eastern Europe where a dispute broke out over who would be the shochet. *The town's air was heavy with acrimony and* lashon hara. *Rav Zev tried his utmost to distance himself from the conflict and slander.*

Rav Zev and his wife agreed that they couldn't remain in the town without being affected by the friction. Even though it was Thursday and Shabbos was coming, they packed their bags and left town. They gave up their successful business, friends, and neighbors and moved away.

Some time after this incident, World War II broke out. The Nazis did not conquer the village Rav Zev had moved to. Unfortunately, his neighbors from his previous town were rounded up and taken to Auschwitz. Only a few people survived.

(Purity of Speech, Lesson 52)

The Chofetz Chaim would travel from city from city selling his seforim. *On one trip he hired a young man to show him the way around a particular city. As they neared one of the houses, the boy pointed and said, "In this house lives a wealthy Jew, but he is very stingy. It's best that we don't even bother knocking on his door."*

As soon as these words were uttered, the Chofetz Chaim paid the boy the full amount he had promised him and sent him away. Lashon hara was so despicable to him that he wanted to have no further contact with someone capable of uttering such a statement. He did not relent even after the young man promised to repent.

(Sefer Meir Enei Yisroel)

The Chofetz Chaim once visited the village of Yadovna to sell his books. He kept his identity as the author of the seforim *a secret, but although he never let on that he was more than a peddler of books, people who fixed their eyes on him could tell that he was special.*

The local shochet *invited him to stay with him for Shabbos. The Shabbos passed in elevated companionship. After Minchah, the Chofetz Chaim prepared to wash for Shalosh Seudos. Suddenly he heard his host say to his wife, "What do you think about the chutzpah of the butcher! A time will come where his lies will trap him. I heard him give his word to Getzel that the last animal I slaughtered was* glatt.*"*

Suddenly the shochet *noticed that his guest had disappeared — gone without a word. When the* shochet *arrived for Maariv and met the Chofetz Chaim, he asked, "Where did you disappear to?"*

The Chofetz Chaim excused himself. "You must remember that I earn a living selling a book that attempts to teach people to be careful to avoid lashon hara. *How could I remain in a house where* lashon hara *and* rechilus *is repeated? If you have a complaint against the butcher, then rebuke him or tell the Rav to speak to him. But who gave you permission to discuss the issue in your house?"*

(*Mayim Chaim, Mishpatim*)

Not listening may be difficult for the first few weeks, but after that you will have established your reputation as a non-listener. Those who regularly speak *lashon hara* will go elsewhere.

Perhaps, if we become really good at it, we may start to resemble Rabbi Shlomo Leib of Lentchna, who was incapable of hearing that which was inappropriate. His ears ceased functioning, even if the words were screamed in his presence. (*Igeres Le'horim*)

Lashon Hara Le'toeles

There are seven rules of repeating negative information that will prevent a person from being victimized. The most important rule to remember: if in doubt as to whether it is *lashon hara* or not — say nothing.

When Rav Shlomo Zalmen Auerbach's sister stopped by to inquire about a shidduch, *Rav Shlomo Zalmen nodded his approval. As she was about to leave, he asked if she was visiting their other sister. She declared her intentions to head there shortly.*

When she arrived at her sister's home, she found her brother there waiting for her. "Tell them not to pursue the shidduch," *he declared.*

He could not reveal his true thoughts in front of his wife, because it would be lashon hara *for her to hear his disparaging comment.*

Two yeshivah students once asked the Chazon Ish whether it was permissible to repeat some information that would normally be considered lashon hara *for a noble purpose. They explained the scenario and the purpose to the Chazon Ish.*

"Even if it is permissible," replied the Chazon Ish, "do you know how to speak the permissible type of lashon hara?"

The Chazon Ish explained his question with an anecdote.

At the first meeting and establishment of the Agudas Yisroel, at which Rav Chaim Soloveitchik was present, a rabbi rose to speak and condemned a certain community activist for some of the things he had done. He pointed out the negative outcomes of the man's choices and decisions and the need to undo them.

The speaker was correct, and his words should have been considered the noble type of lashon hara. Nevertheless, Rav Chaim still rose from his seat and left the auditorium.

What was the problem? Concluded the Chazon Ish, "Rav Chaim felt that the rabbi was enjoying his speech too much. Rather than expressing remorse over the negative events that had occurred, he appeared to relish his role in revealing the damage that had resulted. Had his intentions been purely noble, he would have spoken solemnly: 'Dear rabbis, I regret to inform you of some of the recent failures in our community. Let us correct the wrongdoing.'

"That is the way to speak words of permissible lashon hara."

———

When the Steipler had to say something negative about someone for a beneficial purpose, he used allusions rather than speaking directly. (*Toldos Yaakov*, page 207)

Someone once said something negative about a certain individual who was no longer alive. The Steipler responded by saying, "Why should you speak lashon hara *about someone who is no longer alive?*

The man replied, "I heard the Chazon Ish criticize him one Yom Kippur."

The Steipler retorted, "When he was alive, there was value to speaking out against him. But now that he is dead, it is strictly lashon hara."

(*Toldos Yaakov,* page 207)

Connected Character Traits

It is not enough to study the laws and information on *shmiras ha'lashon.* One must work on correcting the bad character traits that lead to speaking *lashon hara.*

Rav Yeruchem Levovitz used to say that *lashon hara* is defined as a bad tongue; a tongue whose essence is bad because it is guided by negative sources. That tongue's owner must study *mussar* and work on negative *middos,* which will convert the bad tongue into a good tongue.

A person who seeks to acquire the quality of *shemiras ha'lashon* must strengthen his faith and trust so he does not become upset if someone causes him harm or loss. He will remain confident that Hashem will replenish his losses. He will refrain from speaking negatively or feuding with anyone.

Rav Yitzchok Zilberstein once observed a group of men go over to a Torah scholar and inform him that someone had said something negative about him. The laws of shemiras ha'lashon *permitted the sharing of this information, to allow the one being slandered to take necessary action. As he listened to their warning, the Torah scholar turned ashen.*

During the Torah reading he went over to the gabbai *and asked to make a* mi shebeirach *blessing for someone. Everyone was certain he would mention the name of an ill person. But Rav Zilberstein immediately recognized the name as belonging to the individual who had spoken badly of him. The Torah scholar feared that speaking* lashon hara *would hurt the speaker, so he immediately took action to shield him from harm. Such is the behavior of a true son of the King of kings, who seeks only the best for others.*
(*Borchi Nafshi, Bereishis,* page 87)

The various negative character traits that can lead to *lashon hara* are represented in the mnemonic phrase, "*Kol Gehinnom.*"

Anger

The letter *kaf* stands for *kaas*, anger. When a person's anger is aroused he finds it impossible to control his tongue. In the heat of his rage he has no regard even for the Divine Presence. (*Nedarim* 22b)

We are warned to stay far away from a person who gets angry easily. The *Zohar* (*Parshas Tezaveh*) points out that associating with such a person puts us at risk of being contaminated by their debased form which has been altered by the forces of impurity.

Mockery

The letter *lamed* stands for *leitzanus*, mockery. Some people like to constantly tell jokes, which leads them to join gatherings to make fun of others. The *Gemara* points out that scoffers will inevitably make negative statements about others (*Sota* 42a). This negativity will sometimes take the form of laughter.

> *Rav Shlomo Wolbe once gave an exceptionally powerful talk to a group of his student in Yerushalayim. Afterwards, one of his students came forward to thank him. Still reeling under the impact of his words, the student said, "This was such a powerful talk. It is so clear that it is the truth that no one could possibly refute it."*
>
> *"Do you really believe no one can refute it?" said Rav Wolbe. "I can refute it quite readily. Listen: Ha, ha, ha. One word of mockery can counteract one hundred rebukes."*
>
> (Heard from Rav Mattisyahu Salomon)

Pride

The letter *gimmel* stands for *gaavah*, pride. There are those who think they are superior to everyone else and therefore belittle others. Many people feed their pride by speaking badly of others. They cannot tolerate when others are praised. (*Kol Yehudah, Parshas Tazria*) A person who sees another accorded greater honor than he, tells himself, "Were it not for him I would receive greater honor." He then digs until he finds something derogatory.

Ponder the shamefulness of this act, which leads to so many sins. Examine your own character. Are you meeting your own potential? If we are fully aware of our own faults, we will be less likely to speak against others.

Despair

The letter *yud* stands for *ye'ush*, despair. Some people think it's not possible to have a good conversation without speaking *lashon hara*, and they don't even try to restrain themselves. The *yetzer hara* tries to capitalize on these feelings by telling us, "Almost anything you say is considered *lashon hara*, so it doesn't pay to be careful. If you focus on *shemiras ha'lashon*, you won't be able to talk at all!"

Many people feel overwhelmed by the apparent excessive demands of *shemiras ha'lashon*. The fact is, however, that Hashem doesn't give us any commandments that are too difficult to fulfill.

Hopelessness

The letter *heh* stands for *hefker*, hopelessness. Many do not even consider speaking *lashon hara* to be a problem: "Everyone does it, so why should I be different?" They see that others are lax with their speech, and they willingly follow in their footsteps.

This rationale makes no sense. If a person were afflicted with a fatal illness, *Rachmana litzlan*, and heard that a doctor at the other side of the world had discovered a cure, wouldn't he do all within his power to make contact with that doctor? The fact that there were others who were not making the effort would not dissuade him. In the case of *shemiras ha'lashon*, we are talking about making the effort to access eternal life. (*Shemiras Ha'lashon*)

A man wanted to purchase all the seforim *the Chofetz Chaim had written, except for his work on* shemiras ha'lashon. *When asked why he had no interest in the* Sefer Chofetz Chaim, *he explained that he was a businessman who found it difficult to avoid forbidden speech.*

The Chofetz Chaim replied, "It's worth studying, even if the only result is that when you speak lashon hara *it is with a sigh."*

Finding Fault

The letter *nun* stands for *nagranus*, a fault finder. Some people always comment on the faults of others. This type of person is incapable of judging a person favorably. He interprets anything said to him in the negative. Any favors people do for him are viewed as harmful instead of beneficial. He actively doles out evil in exchange for good he has received! This person even sees the good that Hashem sends his way in a negative light. He is by nature ungrateful. (Rabbi Yitzchak Abuhav, *Menoras Ha'maor*)

Permitting the Forbidden

The letter mem stand for *muttar*, permitted. Out of ignorance, a person may believe that is it possible to say something that is actually *lashon hara*. This approach stems from lack of knowledge of the laws.

He may decide that speaking badly of others is permissible because he speaks *lashon hara* so regularly that it has lost its sting in his eyes. When any transgression is no longer viewed as serious, this attitude reduces the person to being a rebel in Hashem's eyes. (Klausenberger Rebbe, *Parshas Toldos* 5730)

Food For Thought

When a person has a kashrus question, he asks a Rav. But when it comes to speaking *lashon hara*, he makes his own halachic decisions to permit that which is forbidden.

(*Yirah Ve'daas*)

Additional character traits that lead a person to speak badly about others are jealousy and hate. According to Rav Chaim Vital, jealousy causes hate. (*Shaarei Kedushah*, Vol. II, Gate 4)

The process whereby this happens can be easily traced. First the person focuses on something the other person has, which he doesn't have. Next comes the thought that he also deserves this thing. Not only that, it would be far better if the object would be in his possession!

In the next stage he sees the possession as his own and wonders how his neighbor came to have it. The final conclusion is that the neighbor is a thief for having taken what is really his.

In essence, being jealous of someone's possessions is the equivalent of declaring that one is unhappy with Hashem's running of the world (Rav Mattisyahu Salomon). The best thing we can do to uproot jealousy is to strengthen our trust in Hashem.

Remembering Miriam's Punishment

"Remember that which the Lord, your G-d, did to Miriam, on the way when you were leaving Egypt" (*Devarim* 24:9).

Be careful not to falsely suspect another person. Remember what Hashem did to Miriam, who falsely suspected Moshe of something that wasn't true — and she was smitten by *tzara'as*. (*Targum Yonasan*)

The Ramban considers remembering what Miriam suffered as one of the 613 mitzvos (Ramban, *Devarim* 24:9). The Alter of Slobodka juxtaposes this remembrance with that of remembering Amalek. Just as the significance of the latter is larger-than-life, so should any association with negative speech loom intolerably on our horizon. (*Ohr Ha'tzafun*) Keep this in the back of your mind as you engage in conversation so you remember to seal your mouth (*Chareidim*, Chapter 9).

There are many considerations that could lead us to conclude that Miriam did not really do any harm when she made her comments concerning Moshe. Rabbeinu Bachya points to the following mitigating factors:

- Miriam was a righteous prophetess.
- She spoke out only against her brother, and only this single time, demonstrating that criticizing others was not a constant aspect of her personality.
- She was older than Moshe.
- She had raised him.
- She had risked her life on his behalf at the Nile.
- She did not speak directly in front of him, to avoid causing him undue embarrassment.
- The Netziv adds that her act was inadvertent and mistaken.
- The Sifri notes that she had Moshe's best interests in mind.

Notwithstanding these many redeeming factors, Hashem punished Miriam with *tzara'as*. The camp did not journey until she recovered, yet her punishment was not deferred. These factors indicate that an extremely grave transgression had taken place.

Ramban argues that if a highly distinguished individual like Miriam, for whom there were so many reasons not to be punished, was given *tzara'as*, how can any of us reasonably expect to be forgiven without any punitive consequence for the transgression of *lashon hara*? (*Hilchos Tumas Tzara'as*, Chapter 16, Halachah 10)

> *A man had two sons, one known to be brilliant and the other a simpleton. The brilliant son was so proud of his accomplishment that he was constantly getting into fights with anyone who appeared to question his authority. His father was greatly humiliated by his bad behavior. To soothe ruffled feelings and to make it clear to everyone that he did not condone his son's behavior, he disciplined him publicly.*
>
> *When the father heard that his simple son was following the same pattern, he spoke to the young man. "When your accomplished brother misbehaved, I did not hesitate to humiliate him publicly. Given your deficiencies, I certainly would not hesitate to discipline you even more stringently if word of any misbehavior on your part were to reach me."*
>
> (Introduction to *Zachor Le'Miriam*)

Because *lashon hara* is such an inherently socially destructive act, it will be treated severely, regardless of who pronounces it and about whom it is said. *Lashon hara* is never overlooked. Those who participate in disseminating it cannot hide behind any special status. They will never succeed in deflecting the blame and accountability for having engaged in malicious gossip.

Both Rashbam and Tosefos Berachah emphasize that we see from the example of Miriam, as well as that of King Uziyahu (see *II Melachim* 26:20), that once someone is afflicted with this skin disease, it must be allowed to take its course. No matter how important and influential the individual suffering from the malady may be, he will have to be segregated from society as long as the condition remains.

Meditate on the seriousness of Miriam's suffering, to stir yourself to a commitment to guard your tongue!

Food For Thought

Rav Simcha Zissel of Kelm wondered why the Torah saw fit to tell us the story of Miriam speaking out against her brother. Isn't the story *lashon hara*? The answer is that it is permissible to repeat any story that will enable people to correct themselves and improve their character.

(*Maamarim Nivcharim* of Rav Yehudah Zev Segal)

"They set their mouths in heaven when their tongues wag on earth" (*Tehillim* 83:9). This verse teaches us that negative comments made here on earth can have a devastating effect on the subject's rating in Heaven.

There is nothing that distances man from his Creator like *lashon hara*.

(*Ohr Ha'Chaim, Vayikra* 14:9)

Many great people would place a small piece of paper on their table with the words, "Remember what was done to Miriam" written on it. (*Zachor Le'Miriam*)

Tzara'as and *Lashon Hara*

When the Jewish People were on a high spiritual level, speaking *lashon hara* resulted in the appearance of white patches on their skin. The commentaries explain that this pathology of dead skin meant to suggest that the life force of speech was being misused.

The word *metzorah* (a person afflicted with *tzara'as*) is short for *motzi shem rah*, he gives [other people] a bad name and brings out the bad [in people] (*Archin* 15b). To provide a deterrent that will discourage people from following the example of the speaker of *lashon hara*, the Torah provided a framework wherein such an individual finds himself disenfranchised from even his inner circle of friends and family when he is afflicted with *tzara'as*.

If the sinner took the message seriously, the temporary *metzorah* might have just a week or two of waiting to see what would develop. Otherwise his *tzara'as* would be fully diagnosed, warranting seclusion until he rectified the underlying spiritual malady. The time spent being restricted to a solitary existence as a result of *tzara'as* will hopefully give the individual pause to reconsider how to attempt to make himself more spiritual in every dimension.

Different manifestations of *tzara'as* reflected a greater need to labor on uprooting the inner corruption inherent in the speaker. Sometimes a person needed weeks to learn how to recalibrate the balance between body and soul, particularly in terms of evaluating one's fellow. He required additional time to master the tools of focusing on the good in others and judging them favorably.

The *metzorah* was forbidden to enter all three camps in the desert. Why is only a *metzorah* singled out to live in isolation? The reason for rehabilitating him in this manner is because he caused a husband to separate from his wife and friends to become distant from one another. (*Archin* 16b) The individual who creates a division between man and his fellow man with his slanderous speech is to be isolated from people, so he will experience the loneliness that he caused. One who disrupts relationships between people should rightfully be subjected to loneliness.

A person who avoids *lashon hara* utilizes the power of speech in a positive way and is perpetually enhancing the spiritual power of his words. The opposite is also true: the prayer of a person who speaks *lashon hara* is tainted and cannot enter the presence of Hashem. Because of this contamination, a *metzorah* would cry "Impure, impure" to others, so they would know of his suffering and daven on his behalf.

A *metzorah* had to tear his clothing and let his hair grow wild because pride induced him to put others down.

Spending time in introspection will reduce his swollen pride, until he sinks to the level of a worm and hyssop. (*Shemiras Ha'lashon II, Tazria-Metzorah*)

After a *metzora* was healed, he was required to bring additional sacrifices beyond the usual lamb required for an ordinary sin offering. He had to offer two birds, wood from a cedar tree, and a red thread. Only afterwards is he forgiven.

The two birds represent the speaker's tendency to twitter nonstop. Instead of exercising restraint, the hallmark of human beings, he has lowered himself to the level of birds. (*Daas Torah*)

Why did his sacrifice require supplementary contributions? Rav Simcha Zissel Ziv of Kelm explained that studying the section of the *metzorah* is compared to visiting a doctor prior to an operation. If the patient sees the doctor preparing many surgical instruments for the procedure, he will become very apprehensive about his upcoming operation. When we learn about all the requirements needed for the purification of the *metzorah*, we should become very uneasy about the corruption caused by *lashon hara*.

As part of Hashem's general withdrawal from our visible everyday surroundings, categorized as *hester panim* (the hiding of the Face), we have lost the ability to receive feedback on our spiritual state of affairs in a most immediate and profound fashion. We are left to rely on our own self-evaluations and the input of trusted and sensitive friends.

In 5608, a cholera epidemic spread across Vilna. As in all troubled times, the Jewish community searched their souls and tried to improve their ways, in the hope that the terrible illness would vanish from their midst.

One man went to Rav Yisroel Salanter to report that grave sins were being committed in a certain individual's home. In response, Rav Yisroel explained to him why a metzorah *was expelled from society.*

Chazal tell us that *tzara'as* in a punishment for *lashon hara*. The reason *lashon hara* is so damaging is not because the perpetrator is spreading lies, but because he is too busy looking for faults in his friend.

> *The message to one who speaks* lashon hara *is this: if you are so good at finding faults, stay outside of the community and do some introspection. Go outside, sit by yourself, and think about your own deeds. Search your own soul for blemishes instead of concentrating on other people's misdoings.*
>
> *(Iturei Torah)*

Teshuvah For Lashon Hara

People tend to regard sins of the mouth as less serious than sins associated with deeds. Because of this, even when they repent their repentance is not truly heartfelt. Yet our Sages have equated this sin with the three most severe sins, and so a person must make the effort to repent and stay away from developing this dangerous habit. (*Shaarei Teshuvah*)

The first step is *regret*. Ponder your own hurt in the past when someone spoke against you. Consider the displeasure caused Hashem by speaking badly against one of His children.

Feel the anguish of having exchanged your merits for someone else's sins. Reflect on the negative impact on your prayers.

Next is *azivas ha'cheit*—abandoning this sin. A woman comments on Sorah's chronic lateness to the others waiting for her arrival so the meeting can begin. Rivkah has a real funny story about Sorah arriving late to an important function, but instead she deftly changes the topic.

Step three is *vidui* — verbal confession of sin. "I wish I had never spoken those terrible words about Avrohom. I lowered his stature in the eyes of those listening to me and I lowered my own stature before Hashem."

Kabbalah le'asid—undertaking not to sin in the future. Studying the laws of *lashon hara* every day is a good way to prevent a repetition in the future. Try to get your peers interested in studying the halachos, so your community will speak less *lashon hara.*

Say the special prayer asking Hashem to help us avoid speaking *lashon hara.* If you have heard something negative about someone, get it out of your system by judging favorably.

> *The Chofetz Chaim would speak of a Rav who would preface each conversation with others with a silent prayer to Hashem to protect him from* lashon hara. *Before visiting Lavan, Yaakov davened for protection from the source of deception and slander—his uncle Lavan.*
>
> (*Zachor Le'Miriam*, Chapter 26, Letter *alef*)

If you find yourself speaking badly about a particular person, avoid mentioning the name of that person. If you find yourself always speaking *lashon hara* to a particular person, study the laws of *lashon hara* with her.

Rav Yehudah Zev Segal recommends a daily review of material relating to *shemiras ha'lashon*, such as that which you are presently reading. This type of information can help you uproot your desire to speak badly of others. By committing oneself to the study of this body of information, one is guaranteed that the Chofetz Chaim will come to his defense.

Even if you have successfully completed the study of Chofetz Chaim many times, it must be continuously studied. That is why Rav Segal implemented the study of two halachos daily, and later asked that the special calendar detailing this commitment be buried with him.

> *Following a lecture on the sinfulness of those who speak* lashon hara, *someone approached the Chofetz Chaim and said, "I know that I have spoken badly of others hundreds of times, but I don't remember the names of the people I spoke about so I cannot ask for their forgiveness. I may also be responsible for influencing others to take this sin lightly. How can I appease the Master of the World?"*
>
> *The Chofetz Chaim replied that one should follow our Sages' advice to use the instrument of sin to appease Hashem (Vayikra Rabbah 21:5). Therefore it is appropriate to learn the halachos and aggados of shemiras ha'lashon in public. This, together with doing the utmost to avoid the sin in the future, will ensure forgiveness.*

The Chofetz Chaim then pointed out that if only everyone would undertake to teach and fulfill, surely Hashem would send Mashiach immediately.

(Kevod Shamayim, Chapter 3)

Educating Children

When children are overheard speaking *lashon hara* they must be stopped. The earlier children are taught to be careful with what they say, the better.

One good way is to set the right example. A parent who speaks *lashon hara* in the presence of his child could just as soon poured hot lead down his throat (*Ohr Yechezkel* letters). Children should never hear a parent speaking badly about others (*Chofetz Chaim*).

It is imperative that educators understand their responsibility to educate their charges to avoid *lashon hara* (Rav Yehudah Zev Segal). The best way to do that is by explaining the importance of the mitzvah of *shemiras ha'lashon*. The teacher must help his student understand how certain sins are of a more serious nature than others.

When Rav Moshe Feinstein was asked if a teacher is permitted to force his students to reveal the perpetrator of a forbidden act, he forbids it. It is best to try to appeal to the child responsible for the deed to come forward on his own and confess. Certainly the obligation to rehabilitate the errant child does not supercede the prohibition against lashon hara.

(Igros Moshe, Yoreh Deah II, Siman 103;
Yoreh Deah IV, Siman 30)

Rav Chaim Friedlander stressed that training in determining priorities should begin early. The Klausenberger Rebbe felt that the concept of *shemiras ha'lashon* should be introduced as soon as a child understands the meaning of words. A young child readily masters the concept of *muktzeh* when his parents shout the word each time he touches something that may not be touched on Shabbos. Whenever the child says something negative, his parents should react with the same vigor. It is their job to ensure that the child recognizes the gravity of both with the same intensity. In this way, as he grows older, one prohibition will be considered as serious as the other. (*Mesilos Ha'Chaim Be'chinuch*)

INSPIRATION

The behavior of an individual who has integrated the principles of *shemiras ha'lashon* is revolutionized (letter of Rav Yehudah Zev Segal). A home where the family members are careful to say only positive things, in a refined matter, is infused with holiness. (*Yirah Ve'daas*)

From cumulative experiences in their formative years, our children will learn that it is possible to enjoy lengthy conversations without speaking badly about others. The Chofetz Chaim was known to be quite a conversationalist.

Judging People Favorably

Judging Ourselves, Judging Others

Each of us regularly demonstrates a remarkable capacity to judge favorably, at least in regard to one person: ourself! If we're late for a meeting, or forgot to do something we promised, we are quick to excuse ourself. But if someone else does the same to us, we find no justification for such rudeness and assume that it reflects how little they care for us.

Just as we excuse ourselves, we must always give others the benefit of the doubt (Rashi, *Vayikra* 19:15; *Samak*; *Shulchan Aruch, Choshen Mishpat* 17:10).

We are sure that our intentions are pure, even when our actions hurt others; but we are unwilling to consider intentions when judging the impact of others' actions on us. We happily sail through life, acknowledging our various shortcomings while remaining confident that we are good people overall. We are not that generous with others, whom we tend to see only in terms of the traits that annoy us.

Many people think that they are much more accomplished than their friends. The reality is that we are all part

261

of a massive assembly line. At General Motors, everyone in the assembly line makes a contribution. Does it make sense for the workforce to argue about which of their jobs is most important? Such a dispute is quite ridiculous — each and every person fulfills a vital role!

What applies to General Motors is also valid about our roles in the real world. If you don't do your job properly, then I can't do mine. All are equally important. The sanctification of Hashem's name is dependent on everyone's input.

The import of each person's contribution is impossible to measure. When a habitual sinner exercises a measure of self-restraint, the sanctification of Hashem's name can be greater than when a righteous person does not sin at all. (*Sefas Emes*)

Revealing the spark of goodness in even the most improper actions of Jews is part of the service of Hashem. No father wants to hear a bad report about his child, even if it is true. A father is extremely appreciative of a person who can find good things to say about his offspring.

This obligation does not require that we find extenuating circumstances to excuse the behavior of a known sinner, a small category of individuals who have, willfully and with full knowledge of their responsibilities, chosen not to identify themselves with the obligations of the Jewish way of life. And when it comes to a completely righteous person, we are to assume that he has no doubt repented or that his acts were justified.

It is those individuals who are not fully righteous or fully wicked that we are obligated to judge favorably. Questionable actions of such people or the community's can be seen in different ways and lend themselves to being judged favorably.

Food For Thought

The ability to overlook, reevaluate, and judge favorably is the precondition for any satisfactory human relationship. Yehoshua ben Perachyah instructs us to acquire a friend and to judge every person favorably (*Avos* 1:6). Without the latter, the former is impossible. And when we see the good in others, they too will view us more positively: "As water reflects a face back to itself, so one's heart is reflected back to him by another" (*Mishlei* 27:19).

When the Torah obligates us to judge others favorably, we are being taught that we must work on changing our thought patterns. To enable us to judge favorably we must get used to seeing others in a positive light, by praising others and acquiring the character traits of Avrohom Avinu: "A good eye, a humble spirit, and an undemanding soul" (*Avos* 5:22).

When the Chofetz Chaim went to the Rav of Lida to ask for an approbation for his Sefer Chofetz Chaim, *the Rav reacted by shouting at the young Rav Yisroel Meir. "How does such a young man dare take upon himself the responsibility of determining the requirements of such difficult halachos? How did you assume that you would be able to familiarize yourself with all the sources, so you could determine* what is permitted and what is forbidden on a topic that is considered the equivalent of the most reprehensible sins?" he angrily declared.

The Chofetz Chaim was deeply saddened by the Rav's reaction. Outside, he met the Rav's brother, who was a Dayan in the city. The Dayan tried to comfort him. "Don't take it too badly; my brother tends to stormy reactions."

Rav Yisroel Meir shook his head. "If he became angry, it was certainly justified. Who am I to have occupied myself with such critical matters? Perhaps it was wrong to undertake such a complicated project. And if his words were uttered in anger, our Sages have said, 'A Torah scholar who gets angry — it is because the Torah he has studied makes him passionate' (Taanis 7a). He struck out at me for Hashem's honor and I appreciate and value his words!"

Such was the Chofetz Chaim's evaluation of the Rav who had just discarded the fruit of his labors with a flick of his hand, and poured scorn on his comprehensive study of shemiras ha'lashon. He judged him favorably and refused to listen to any criticism.

The Dayan walked into his brother's study and repeated his conversation with the Chofetz Chaim. When the Rav heard how the young Rav Yisroel Meir had responded to his criticism, he sent for the Chofetz Chaim and asked for a copy of the sefer so he could study it. He later gave an enthusiastic approbation.

> *Within his wholehearted endorsement is a reference to this episode: "The Rav, the author, speaks well and fulfills his words equally as well."*
>
> *(Darkei Mussar 151)*

> *Reb Aharon of Belz would never refer to a Jew as a sinner or describe him as wicked, even if he had strayed very far. He was incapable of expressing anything negative about anyone. He would portray these impious individuals as Jews of frail character or as one who did not wear the tefillin of Rabbeinu Tam.*

Try stepping out of yourself and seek to justify others' deeds as you would justify, excuse, and understand the extenuating circumstances for your own actions. Look for the other side of the story. Remember that you don't know what is really going on in anyone's life.

We expect others to divine our personal history, know what makes us angry, and understand our idiosyncratic sense of humor. But when it comes to judging others, we forget that we are frequently in the position of someone who starts a novel at chapter three without knowledge of the character's background. Far more often than we imagine, our evaluations of others are totally off the mark—based on missing information, hasty assumptions, or misunderstandings.

We must judge others not on the basis of an isolated act, but in the context of their entire being: judging others as whole beings, not in terms of one trait; constantly reexamining our judgments of others to see if there is another way to view a particular event; looking at interactions from the other person's point of view. This approach enriches our relationships and our lives.

> *The Sefas Emes was very careful when speaking of his fellow Jews, especially the least worthy of them, for fear of uttering a negative word that might arouse a stern echo in the Heavenly Court. When he returned from medical treatment in Berlin, his brother asked if he had found many Jews who conscientiously obey the commandments of Hashem. He replied with an explanation of the injunction to judge every person on the side of merit. (Avos 1:6)*
>
> *He explained, "The phrase says 'kol ha'adam,' literally 'the whole man,' that is, complete with all the conditions and circumstances in which he is placed. And if this is true of a person, how much more so it must be true regarding a multitude. Now to your question: The Jews of Berlin in general, taking into account the conditions and circumstances that surround them, are to be judged favorably."*
>
> *(Rebbes of Ger)*

Changing The Focus

The *yetzer hara* is referred to as an observer (*Tehillim* 37:32). He is like an observer standing in a watchtower with binoculars in his hand. These binoculars can make something far away appear closer, and it can make things up close appear to be a long way off.

The *yetzer hara* makes good use of these binoculars. When we see our friend doing something that is not up to par, he makes it appear far worse than it is. When we do something positive, he makes it appear far greater than it actually was. And if we sin at his instigation, he turns the binoculars the wrong way—making it appear insignificantly small.

Turn the binoculars the other way around! When it comes to others' deeds we are commanded to judge them favorably, and certainly not to enlarge on the wicked aspects of their actions. When it comes to our good deeds, if we truly hold them up to scrutiny, we will surely find many flaws. This ensures that we will never become haughty. (*Shem Olam*, Part II, Chapter 3)

> *In his discourse before Kol Nidrei, Rav Yoel Kluft pointed out that the sure way to extricate ourselves from judgment and convert justice to compassion is to demonstrate the merit of the Jewish People. He explained that he had learned this from his rebbe, the Chofetz Chaim.*
>
> *One year before Kol Nidrei, the Chofetz Chaim focused on the verse, "The entire family of Yisrael shall be forgiven and the convert that lives among them, for all the nation has erred unintentionally." He painted a picture of an elderly goy who decided to convert in his old age, eagerly embracing the yoke of Torah and mitzvos. Despite his earnest dedication to Judaism, he somehow commits a sin.*
>
> *Certainly we would be very understanding! After all, he hasn't had a chance to study much; he has very little experience tucked under his belt. Not having withstood many challenges that build up resistance to*

the yetzer hara, *he hasn't had adequate time to form good habits that would assist him in the performance of mitzvos. Even though he is now a full-fledged Jew, we certainly would not hold his one lapse against him.*

Then the Chofetz Chaim began to cry, "And what about us? How much do we know? How much have we studied? When can be expected from us? May Hashem forgive all of us in the same way that the convert is forgiven, for we are all unintentional sinners."

At this elevated moment before Kol Nidrei on Yom Kippur, the Chofetz Chaim chose to speak words of favorable judgment on behalf of the Jewish People.

(*Daas Yoel*, page 75)

Food For Thought

We are enjoined not to judge another until you are in his place. Since we can never be in his place, we cannot possibly judge him.

(Rav Azriel Mayer Eiger of Lublin)

People do make mistakes, but we should still view them in a positive light. We are commanded to love them and care for them in spite of their mistakes, and to make the effort to emerge with a favorable judgment.

The blessings of Rav Ben Zion Abba Shaul were known to work miracles. Once when he was asked why his blessings were more effective than those of others, he answered, "Because I truly love people."

One evening somebody seriously offended the Rosh Yeshivah. The next morning, one of the yeshivah staff asked him if he had said the customary tefillah *recited before going to sleep, forgiving anyone who had insulted him.*

"I found it very hard to excuse his behavior," the Rosh Yeshivah admitted, "yet I couldn't go to sleep without forgiving him. So I thought over the issue for a long time, trying to judge him favorably. When I was certain that I no longer bore a grudge against him, I recited the tefillah *of forgiveness and went to sleep."*

INSPIRATION

"And You, Holy One, are enthroned on the praises of Yisrael" (*Tehillim* 22:4). Hashem looks for the praises of the Jewish People. He seeks individuals who see no evil in the Jewish People, the ones who "perceived no iniquity in Yaakov" (*Bamidbar* 23:21). Hashem is at the side of such a virtuous individual.

(*Divrei Chaim*)

Only Hashem can truly judge a person. Unfortunately we have a tendency to assume the worst. We think, "How irresponsible he is," and, "She was so thoughtless." We tend to make decisions based on very limited information and biased by our own personal belief systems.

If something has happened before, it's easy to assume that similar circumstances will always lead to the same results.

The reality is that they don't. We tend to look with "tunnel vision," seeing only what we want to.

> *While waiting at the airport, a woman observed a family with many fine-looking children. As she watched the family, she noticed an older man hurrying towards them. The accusations he leveled against the father of the children were so loud and vehement that the woman easily overheard them.*
>
> *"What have you done? You fled in middle of the night, taking my daughter and grandchildren. You didn't even let me kiss them goodbye. And this was after I made you a rich man!"*
>
> *The woman listening felt compassion for this wounded grandfather, wronged by an ungrateful son-in-law.*
>
> *How different our assessment of the situation is when we are reminded that this was exactly what took place when Lavan caught up with Yaakov, after he fled Lavan's home to return to the land of his fathers.*

Food For Thought

Rav Simcha Zissel Ziv Broida used to joke, "Why was man's mind created with a tinge of crookedness?" He answered, "To judge one's fellow man favorably, one must sometimes twist his mind."

(*Prince of the Torah Kingdom*, page 444)

The Belzer Rebbe, Reb Aharon, labored mightily to judge each Jew favorably. He would say, "Just as one toils to understand a difficult Rambam, so must one work hard to find a merit for a fellow Jew." He would quote his grandfather, Rav Yehoshua of Belz, who said, "I like the pilpul approach to the study of the Talmud. Sometimes we must avail ourselves of this type of convoluted approach to get at a means of judging someone favorably."

Jealousy And Criticism

People often condemn others out of jealousy and hate. When a person observes that his friend is more successful than he is, jealousy stirs within. One way to soothe his turbulent emotions is to persuade himself that his friend achieved success through falsehood and deceit.

People who feel rather unexceptional seek to exalt their status by being critical of others. This serves to bring their peers down to their level.

Food For Thought

If a person sees a flaw or blemish in another Jew, it is proof that he has the identical flaw, for it is like a person looking into a mirror. Just as one sees a dirty face reflected in a mirror when his own face is dirty, a person who is always fault-finding does so because he sees his own faults. He sees his friend as a reflection of himself.

(*Meor Einayim, Chukas*)

When we identify a negative trait in others, it is a signal to us to be extra cautious. It is likely that this negative trait is really inside us, too, and we are just unaware of it. Our sensitivity to another person's flaws often arises out of our dislike for the same flaw within ourselves.

This is why it is inappropriate to discuss other people's flaws, even for a constructive purpose, when we ourselves possess the same flaws. The first order of priority is to fix ourselves. Then we can see others in a clear, true light. (Chofetz Chaim)

The habit of reflexively criticizing others, whether it is individuals with whom we are in contact or members of other societal groups, exacts a heavy price. When our Sages taught that jealousy, the pursuit of physical pleasure, and the quest for honor drive a person from the world, they meant this world. To the extent that we see others as competitors for pieces of a limited pie of material goods, and someone else's gain as our loss, everyone we meet becomes a potential enemy. Turning a jaundiced eye on one and all is truly a recipe for making life utterly distasteful.

Food For Thought

When a person condemns his friend in judgment, he transgresses both the commandments to judge favorably and to love your friend as yourself. In all likelihood he also transgresses "You shall not hate your brother in your heart." (Rambam, *Hilchos Deios*; *Magen Avrohom, Orach*

Chayim 256; *Archin* 16b) When we judge favorably, showing compassion for our fellow Jews, we imitate the *middos* of Hashem, fulfilling the obligation, "And you shall
cleave to Him" (*Shabbos* 133b; *Sota* 14a; *Hilchos Deios*).

A school principal relates how he lost out because he focused on the negative aspects of a teacher's behavior:

> *I have always been able to get along with all my
> teachers, except for one who stood out for his disor-
> derliness. His paperwork was a disaster. Rules and
> regulations played no role in his teaching methodol-
> ogy. Whenever I introduced any new requirements,
> he always conveniently forgot.*
>
> *I would have fired him long ago, except for the
> fact that all his students excelled. Even those who
> were doing poorly in other classes did extremely
> well under his tutelage. The parents loved him, too.
> At every PTA meeting, I was constantly hearing his
> praises sung.*
>
> *As our student body increased, our building be-
> came very overcrowded. When I heard that a well-
> known philanthropist wanted to donate a substan-
> tial amount of money to a school for the elevation of
> his parents' souls, I arranged for him to visit our ye-
> shivah.*
>
> *In anticipation of the meeting, I gathered all the
> teachers together and informed them that the phi-
> lanthropist would be visiting each class. I asked that*

they make an extra effort to ensure that all the classes were sparkling clean and that the children showed proper respect for the visitor. The teacher with no understanding of the word responsibility was, of course, also present.

Sometime earlier, he had made a deal with his class that if they learned industriously and completed the tractate they were studying, they would be rewarded with a prize. What was the prize? A bumper-car activity! They would turn over their seats and wield them like bumper cars, crashing them into one another. The students knew they could rely on their rebbi *to give them a good time, so they studied hard and performed very well on their exam.*

On the day the philanthropist visited the school, I took him from class to class. He was very impressed by the serious learning taking place and the orderliness and cleanliness we encountered. That is, until we reached the classroom of my pet-peeve teacher.

When I opened the door, I thought I would have a heart attack. All the seats were turned upside down. Some children were crashing into one another, and others were rolling on the floor — with the rebbi *sitting in the middle, directing traffic. Sure enough, this was the day the* rebbi *had decided to reward his students with the time of their lives.*

I could feel my face turn white as I began apologizing for the scene. The rebbi *calmly stood up, dusted himself off and also expressed his apologies for* the disarray in the room. But my mind was made up. This was absolutely the last straw.

When the philanthropist left, I called the rebbi over and let him know that he was fired. "You destroyed all our prospects for a new building. Do you know how long I have been working on nurturing this relationship?"

The rebbi excused himself. "I forgot the visit was today. I'm sorry."

I was livid. "You forgot? That's no excuse. You've ruined our chances of expanding. I don't want to see you ever again."

The rebbi begged me to reconsider. "I have ten children. You will be leaving them without a source of sustenance."

"I don't care!" I shouted. "After the damage you caused me I don't owe you anything."

The rebbi realized that I wasn't going to back down. He collected his things and left.

The next day my son fell and broke his leg. A day later another child crashed into a window and required numerous stitches. When another child had to be hospitalized because she couldn't move her head, and my wife slipped and broke her arm and leg, I knew that these incidents were not a coincidence.

I went to a prominent Rav and told him what had been happening. The Rav's first question was, "Have you hurt anyone lately?" I could only hang my head in shame. After a few moments, I told the story of the visit of the philanthropist.

"What you did was deplorable," the Rav said. "Call the rebbi *and ask for forgiveness. Make sure he pardons you, for it is a matter of life and death."*

The rebbi *readily forgave me. But when I asked him to return to school, he explained that he had already found a job elsewhere.*

But that's not the end of the story. The philanthropist contacted me a few days later, and asked if we could get together so he could give me the funds for the new building. When we met, he told me how impressed he had been by our school.

"I've visited other schools that are very well run, but I didn't like their rigidity. What made your school stand out above the rest was the informality I observed. When I saw that class with the chairs turned upside down, and the rebbi *sitting on the floor with the children, I knew I had found the right place. That's what an ideal classroom should look like!"*

(Told by Rav Yitzchok Silberstein)

Changing Perspectives

In a class given by Rebbetzin Yehudis Samet, two ladies staged an encounter at a grocery store that ended with harsh words exchanged. The audience was asked to evaluate the scenario they had just observed and to name which of the two protagonists were at fault. A portion of the audience laid the blame squarely on the shoulders of the grocery store owner, while others faulted the customer.

Why were reactions so different? People filter their experiences through their specialized life-experience lens, focusing on different details based on their existing attitudes and expectations. Personal character traits play a major role in the interpretation of events. You automatically translate everything you see and hear in relation to your preexisting outlook.

It therefore follows that if someone repeats a story, wouldn't it be foolish to accept their portrayal of events as interpreted by their own personal expectations?

Food For Thought

The Chofetz Chaim wrote, "A person should try to perfect his character so he can be counted among the worthy, and not the unworthy. What are the traits of the worthy? They help others whenever they are able; they conceal other people's weaknesses, as they would their own. And if they see a person angry at another, they try to calm him, by giving him an understanding of the other person's position."

(Shemiras Ha'lashon)

First we must admit that our negative judgments are based on conjectures, partial truths and insufficient evidence. Then we must replace our negative judgments with positive ones. Familiarizing ourselves with as many stories about judging favorably as we can will enlarge our repertoire of ideas. The more possibilities we can conjure up, the more likely that we will have plausible explanations available for behaviors that at first glance appear negative. The truth may end up being even more outlandish than your conjectures.

Food For Thought

What do you think when you see someone doing something wrong?

- Perhaps the circumstances rendered the action permissible
- He didn't realize the action was forbidden
- Perhaps the action was accidental
- His *yetzer hara* was so strong that he couldn't help himself
- He didn't mean it that way
- His words were quoted out of context
- The person who gave you this information may be mistaken or hypercritical
- The biggest *limud zechus* nowadays is that the world around us is so perverted
- Because all souls are not equal, some people have bigger challenges than others. You cannot be sure you would have performed better in similar circumstances.
- Who knows how many times he's been hurt by others?

Rav Yaakov Kamenetsky and his wife were once caught in a dreadful storm. Using the lightning as their guide, they cautiously moved towards a house visible in the distance. They were overjoyed when they noticed a mezuzah on the doorpost. But to their horror, the Jewish homeowner refused to allow them to enter. He would not even permit them to step into his vestibule; he simply slammed the door in their faces.

You can well imagine the distress of Rav Yaakov and his wife, standing in the frightening downpour with no roof over their heads. Rav Yaakov certainly had to work hard to activate his favorable judgment tools. And imagine his amazement when the man received an important honor in shul the next morning!

Rav Yaakov later discovered that right before they had arrived, the man's house had been emptied of its valuables by a previous guest.

INSPIRATION

Before birth a person is warned that he should be a righteous person and not a wicked person. The words of this warning lend themselves to another interpretation. Read another way, they counsel us to judge others favorably—thereby raising the other person to the status of a tzaddik, a righteous individual.

(*Kli Yakar*)

A person with love in his heart will always find ways to justify the deeds of a friend. This principle is demonstrated in *Parshas Kedoshim*: "And I shall concentrate My attention on that man and upon his family" (*Vayikra* 20:5). Rashi asks, "Why is the family held responsible for the heinous deeds of one of its members?" He explains that a family that includes a tax collector will cover up for him. (*Shavuos* 39) Why? Because love covers up all sins. If only we felt enough love for our fellow man, it would obscure all his sins from our vision.

The Ramban's advice is to pray on behalf of our friends, asking Hashem to supply them with all that they lack. The spiritual energy invested in those prayers makes it difficult to later belittle these individuals. Rav Moshe Chaim Luzatto points out that we should all seek to benefit our generation by praying on its behalf, seeking atonement for those who require it, attempting to bring our fellow Jews to repentance, and advocating on their behalf before Hashem (*Mesilas Yesharim* 19).

Avoid Seeing Evil In Others

The discussion of things positive raises our spiritual level; discussing the negative lowers it.

The *yetzer hara* has many reasons for inducing a person to speak badly about others. When you discuss another person's misdeeds, your negative feelings about the deed begin to disappear. It takes on a veneer of acceptability, until you actually repeat it! (*Chovos Ha'talmidim*)

> *When a Jew was fleeing to a city of refuge, he never had to ask for directions. There were numerous signs showing the way. Hashem did not want the murderers stopping to ask for directions and discussing the details of their deed. For the concept loses its severity in the repetition, and the embarrassment associated with that misdeed is lessened. No longer could one make the statement that a Torah-observant Jew does not act this way! Discussing it makes it more likely that the evil deed will be repeated.*
>
> (*Maharil Diskin*)

When we judge a person favorably we create a *kiddush Hashem*. Hashem's name is sanctified by converting something negative into positive.

When we see someone doing something that appears negative, we can choose what to focus on. We can think and speak about the negative aspects or the positive aspects of the various people we know. Focusing on the evil in others submerges us in their negativity and poisons our surroundings. Surrounding ourselves with negative judgments has a negative impact on us and our environment. (*Notzar Chesed*, Chapter 4)

> *When Chaim joined a new minyan, he was disturbed to see an older man—one who was well-liked and highly respected by the congregation—davening faster than the speed of light. Chaim had never seen anyone daven at such a pace. The others had barely begun, and he was already taking three steps back and completing the last words of Shemoneh Esrei.*
>
> *Chaim tried to come up with different excuses for the man's behavior. Perhaps he had to hurry home due to some crisis. Perhaps he had a lot on his mind. But as the days went by, it became harder and harder to come up with an excuse to justify this unusual behavior.*
>
> *For lack of any alternative, Chaim decided to ask the elderly man why he devoted only a number of minutes each morning to his tefillos. The man was gracious enough to share his story—which Chaim found to be both astounding and inspirational.*
>
> *When he was a young man during World War II, the man was in a camp surrounded by sadistic*

guards. "It was a capital offense to be caught davening. No questions were asked; the offender was promptly shot then and there.

"Despite all the risks, I was determined to somehow daven each day. This was the one mitzvah that still connected me with the Ribono shel Olam, and I was determined to stick to it at all costs.

"I found a deep pit where I could hide each morning and daven before the morning roll call. How I cherished those moments hiding in the pit, when I could pour out my heart to Hashem. My tormentors had taken everything from me — even my name! But they could never sever my bond with Hashem.

"I knew I was risking my life. Every moment increased the danger. I became accustomed to davening quickly — very quickly — for my life was hanging by a thread.

"When peace finally came, I had been praying quickly for so long that it had become a firmly entrenched habit. I couldn't slow down the pace. That's why I still daven today with the same concentrated speed."

The man shrugged his shoulders ruefully, as though apologizing for his unusual habit. "I'm sure Hashem hears my tefillos as I say them. Even after the war, I have never missed a tefillah."

Chaim listened in awestruck silence. What a radical turnabout! A man who seemed to lack proper respect for tefillah had actually risked his life each day for two full years in order to daven to Hashem.

(*Kovetz Sipurim*, Vol. IV)

A car stopped not far from Rav Yitzchok Silberstein in Ramat Chein on Shabbos, and the driver called out a request for directions. The Rav was quite annoyed. What chutzpah — to stop someone who was clearly religious to request directions on Shabbos!

As he walked towards the driver, intent on giving him a piece of his mind, he saw a stethoscope hanging around his neck and a doctor's bag at his side. Rav Silberstein suddenly realized that the doctor was on a mission of mercy.

After this incident, Rav Silberstein was more readily able to judge others favorably. He recalled that he had heard that the Belzer Rebbe, Reb Aharon, would shout, "Mazel tov, mazel tov!" at passing cars on Shabbos, with the assumption that the reason for the trip was an imminent birth.

(Aleinu Le'shabeiach, Vayikra, page 198)

EXERCISE

For one week try to keep a record of all the times you were critical of others. Review your list and consider if there is any way you can reevaluate those judgments. Ask yourself if you were ever guilty of any of the same actions. Think of incidents when you were able to justify your own behavior, but judged others harshly for the same actions.

Consider these typical examples:

- Your neighbor bypasses you in the street without acknowledging your presence. "Is it so hard to say hello? What a snob!"

- A neighbor refuses to lend you something. "How self-ish! Why couldn't she lend it to me?"
- Your children go to a neighbor to play, but she turns them away. "When her children come here I always let them play."
- Your friend arrives late for an appointment and doesn't even ask for forgiveness. "What nerve!"

Have you ever been guilty of similar behavior? What excuse did you find for yourself? Now reconsider your reaction to your friend's behavior. What excuse can you find for her?

It can be very difficult to judge someone favorably when he does something that angers you. In a calm moment, think about the people you interact with on a regular basis and review the negative acts they engage in that are likely to annoy you. Try judging them favorably in advance of the deed. Then, when you are later challenged by their negative behavior, you will be able to use the excuses you have already prepared.

EXERCISE

Try judging someone favorably once a day for a week. Do not put the exploit out of your mind until you succeed in finding a positive justification for the deed. The next week try to judge two people favorably each day.

What do you do if your adversary is a family member? How do you deal with a close relative who is making your life miserable?

After hearing a lecture about judging people favorably, a woman raised her hand and told Rabbi Noach Weinberg, "Rabbi, the ideas you shared are very nice, but you don't have my sister-in-law in your life.

"Every time I leave the room she stabs me in the back. She never has a nice thing to say about anyone. How can I possibly deal with her?"

Rabbi Weinberg answered, "Imagine you're standing at an intersection, waiting for the light to change. Sudden someone behind you shoves you into the street. You fall on your face and struggle to your feet, all scratched and dirty. You turn, ready to give the person who shoved you a piece of your mind. You open your mouth—and then you discover that the person behind you is wearing dark glasses and holding a white cane.

"How do you feel now? You calm down, and your anger instantly turns to pity. He couldn't help it. He's blind.

"That," Rabbi Weinberg continued, "is your sister-in-law. She's blind. She doesn't wake up in the morning and decide to hurt people that day. She literally doesn't know what she is doing. Instead of anger, have pity."

Rabbi Weinberg concluded by giving everyone a useful tool. "The next time your parent, in-law,

coworker, or neighbor does or says something un-
believably cutting, picture them wearing dark
glasses and holding a white cane. They are blind.
They can't see that they are doing wrong. Help
them, guide them, and gently show them the error
of their ways.

"But don't expect them to change immediately. A
blind person can't see overnight. It takes time, and
sometimes they will never see. Feel sorry for them."

Of course, judging favorably does not preclude action. We must take action when necessary to prevent abuse, while at the same time keeping an open mind to possibilities we are unaware of. If you can change a situation to protect yourself, you certainly must take action to do so.

The Benefits Of Judging Favorably

Offering a plausible explanation for the seemingly negative behavior of others helps diffuse destructive speech. It also makes us less likely to get angry and helps us avoid grudge-bearing and even hatred and disputes.

Hashem has little tolerance for those who speak ill of others. Because Moshe suggested that the Jewish People would not listen to him, he was punished with *tzara'as*. Yeshaya is dealt with severely for referring to the Jewish People as a nation with impure lips (*Yevamos* 49). Highlighting the shortcomings of Klal Yisroel causes distress to Hashem (*Midrash Rabbah, Shemos*).

Gideon's defense of the Jewish People serves as a model for how every Jew should attempt to speak favorably about his fellow man. Gideon says to the angel who appears to him, "Hashem has forsaken us! If our forefathers were righteous, then He should save us in their merit. If they were not deserving, then just as He saved them despite their lack of merit, so should He save us even though we are sinners" (*Shoftim* 6:12–14; see Rashi).

Hashem is pleased by such advocacy on behalf of the Jewish People, and an angel reveals himself to Gideon right after he judges his generation favorably.

Why was it so important for Gideon to verbalize his positive assessment of his generation? After all, the thoughts and deeds of every person are revealed to Hashem! This is clear proof that our judgmental formula is significant.

> *An episode in the Gemara brings another proof of this fact. Rava asked Eliyahu the prophet how Hashem spends His time. He was told that Hashem goes through the lectures of the* Tannaim — *except for those of Rav Meir. Rava realized that Rav Meir's teachings were rejected because he had remained a student of the apostate Acher. He rushed to Rav Meir's defense, noting that Rav Meir eats the fruit and discards the peel; that is, he is capable of sifting the beneficial from the detrimental.*
>
> *Eliyahu then told Rava that at that moment, Hashem was repeating the teachings of Rav Meir. Rava's validation below had an immediate impact on the heavens above.*
>
> (*Tiferes Shlomo*)

Food For Thought

Whoever judges his friend favorably is judged favorably Above.

(Shavuos 30)

If a person regularly judges people favorably and speaks well of them, he becomes a conduit for all things holy.

(Chareidim)

Our Sages cite several examples of people who judged favorably. Each account ends with the words, "May Hashem judge you with favor just as you have judged me with favor."

(Shabbos 127b)

The way in which Hashem judges man is reflective of the way in which the individual acts towards his fellow. Our input plays a major role in the verdict of the Heavenly Court. (*Bris Avrohom*) When we are being judged above, Hashem shows us a friend conducting himself in a similar manner and waits for our evaluation. If we are disapproving and denounce him, then we in turn are condemned; if we are forgiving and judge him favorably, we are also declared guiltless. (*Pri Chayim* 37)

When we judge favorably, Hashem actively focuses on the positive aspects of our deeds (*Shemiras Ha'lashon, Shaar Ha'tevunah* 4). Even if only one out of a thousand angels testifies to our innocence, Hashem will save us if we have zeroed in on the positive in our interpretation of other people's deeds.

The merit of this mitzvah colors the evaluation of our other mitzvos. Hashem readily moves us into the category of righteous because of our righteous outlook.

Food For Thought

The Baal Shem Tov explained the verse "Do not extend your hand with the wicked to be a venal witness" (*Shemos* 23:1) as a reference to joining your testimony to that of the *yetzer hara*. A second witness lends substance to an accusation. The Ozerover Rebbe points out that the *yetzer hara* rises to testify as soon as a person sins, but Hashem rejects that testimony unless another corroboration from below works its way upwards. Who want to be a party to condemning a fellow Jew?

(*Keser Shem Tov*; *Rishfei Kodesh*)

Hashem acts as if He were our shadow. If we embrace compassion, then Hashem is compassionate with us. If we are judgmental, Hashem judges us harshly. When Hashem hears our critical judgment of others, He zeroes in on our own roster of deeds to see if we are guilty of the same or similar acts.

When we declare another person's deed to be outright theft, Hashem looks into our hearts to see if there is any deception within. Do we start daydreaming when the boss moves on? Do we place the

expensive pen in our pocket without making an at-
tempt to seek out the owner? Do we pass off other
people's accomplishments as our own? Do we exag-
gerate when we tell a story? Woe to us for having
launched this type of investigation into our own
deeds. Who will emerge unscathed?

(*Kedushas Levi, Parshas Beshalach*)

Food For Thought

When a person comes forward to defend the Jewish
People, his words may bring salvation for his fellow Jews.
How fortunate such a person is. How great is his merit!

(Damesek Eliezer, *Sanigoria*)

One of the deeds for which reward is given in this
world, while the principal reward is reserved for the
World to Come, is judging someone favorably.

Our morning prayers list several precepts that
fall into this category: honoring one's father and
mother, acts of kindness, early attendance at the
house of study in morning and evening, hospitality
to guests, visiting the sick, providing for a bride, es-
corting the dead, absorption in prayer, bringing
peace between man and his fellow and between man
and his wife. Rashi explains that bringing peace is
an extension of judging favorably.

(*Shabbos 127*)

Which takes precedence, the obligation to rebuke or judging favorably?

Ultimately the goal of everything we do is to bring ourselves and others close to Hashem. Effective rebuke begins by showing our empathy, by making an earnest attempt to understand the other person's motives, by seeing through his eyes, listening to him and comprehending how he view matters in light of his own experiences. In other words, our most effective rebuke will work precisely because we judge others favorably.

Only when we can listen to the rationale of the other person and understand how his experiences, deductions, feelings, and pressures led him to his present state, will we be able to offer words of rebuke that will be accepted. (Rabbeinu Yosef ben Shushan)

Finding merit for one's fellow Jews will evoke the gratitude of Hashem and bring blessing and success on that person, on us and our nation. If only we could.